CYCLING
RIGHTS

KNABE LAW FIRM L.P.A.

14222 MADISON AVENUE
LAKEWOOD, OH 44107

216-228-7200
WWW.KLFOHIO.COM

ISBN: 978-1-63385-509-0

Designed and published by
Word Association Publishers
205 Fifth Avenue
Tarentum, Pennsylvania 15084

www.wordassociation.com
1.800.827.7903

CYCLING
RIGHTS

—*SECOND EDITION*—

KENNETH J. KNABE
GREATER CLEVELAND'S BIKE ATTORNEY
WITH LISA PARKER GREEN

WORD ASSOCIATION PUBLISHERS
www.wordassociation.com
1.800.827.7903

FOREWORD

by Mark J. Looney

CYCLING RIGHTS' SECOND EDITION zeros in exclusively on cycling! New chapters include group riding, children riding, Northeast Ohio bike clubs, the Ohio Bicycle Federation (OBF), and the Ohio to Erie Trail (OTET). These additions along with numerous updates to existing chapters benefit the beginner, intermediate, and advanced cyclist.

Ken masterfully navigates the legal and practical aspects of safe cycling.

And Greater Cleveland's bike scene continues to expand as a premier destination for cyclists with an ever-growing network of bike paths including the Red-Line Greenway, Cleveland's Opportunity Corridor, the Wendy Park Bridge, the OTET terminus in Wendy Park, and the completion of Cleveland's Towpath Trail at Canal Basin Park in the Flats. Since taking his oath of office on January 3, 2022, Cleveland's Mayor Justin M. Bibb has shown, among his numerous initiatives, strong enthusiasm for and commitment to making Cleveland "one of the best bike-friendly cities in the country"! We sincerely hope Mayor Bibb will keep that promise and advocate for safer infrastructure and safety for cyclists.

My Cleveland bike travels included group rides with Ken on the OTET from Cleveland to Cincinnati in 2018 and from Cincinnati to Cleveland in 2022. With his emphasis on safety and injury prevention we completed both our missions all in one piece, with zero injuries or close calls.

Ken's new chapter on group riding is a **must**! Covering the rules, equipment, and etiquette applicable to both seasoned and less experienced cyclists, this chapter offers guidance including how to stay visible, predictable, dependable, and safe! Another new chapter guides adults who are helping children build a strong foundation for bike safety.

Cyclists still face tough issues, situations, and decisions, and this second edition of *Cycling Rights* answers even more pressing questions related to cycling. I travel the country by bicycle, greatly comforted by the knowledge that I have friends such as Ken working to make our cycling byways safe. I carry his phone number in my jersey. If you run into Ken at an upcoming cycling event, be sure to reach out and introduce yourself. You may hear about some of his other new and exciting cycling safety projects.

Mark J. Looney,

Author of *A Path Through Ohio, A Cyclist's Guide to The Ohio to Erie Trail (Third Edition)* and a forthcoming book about cycling around the Great Lakes; Former Member, Board of Director, and Advisor for the Ohio to Erie Trail; Trans-Am Soloist 1983; Director of Quality, Raytheon (Retired); Winner of Buffalo Marathon 1998 & 1999.

AUTHOR'S PREFACE

by Ken Knabe

WE HAD OUR BIKE BOOM (with accompanying bike shortages) during the pandemic, but bike shops are stocked up again. We need to utilize the cycling momentum started during the pandemic by uniting the big three–bike organizations, bike clubs, and bike shops–into one powerful force for laws that protect cyclists and other vulnerable road users.

We need equal rights to safer roads with more driver education on cycling rights, bike favorable infrastructure, and laws that protect us **and** punish careless drivers with increased penalties. We need enhanced police education, and greater enforcement, with citations to all drivers who harass us, hit us, or drive while distracted.

Can you imagine the power if bike orgs, clubs, and shops banded together? Let's do it! If you are a cyclist who wants change, become a member and support one or more of these three categories. Start by joining Bike Cleveland!

Please remember no matter what level rider you are, we are **all** in this together. The preeminent question is, what's the most important factor? The answer is **safety** . . . hence this book and this request that you join one or more of these organizations.

This second edition of *Cycling Rights* offers additional guidance and insight as you navigate the roads or trails from the saddle of your bike.

Many thanks for their invaluable contributions to: Lisa Parker Green of Parker Mulholland LLC[I] for continued editing and writing expertise; Keith Berr and Linda Barberic of Keith Berr Productions[II] for photographic excellence (including a new cover!); Bike Cleveland's Executive Director Jacob VanSickle, Communications & Events Manager Jason Kuhn, Education and Outreach Manager Diana Hildebrand, Advocacy & Policy Manager Jenna Thomas,[III] and Jerrod Amir Shakir, Community Organizer; Cleveland cyclist, MidTown Cleveland Executive Director, former Ohio City Incorporated CEO/Director of Neighborhood Planning, and Vision Zero Cleveland advocate Ashley Shaw; City of Cleveland Senior Strategist, Transit and Mobility and Vision Zero Cleveland advocate Calley Mersmann; author Mark J. Looney (*A Path Through Ohio*);[IV] professional illustrator Matt McLaughlin of Sheffield Lake for exceptional artwork including the new and noteworthy sun glare hazard images;[V] Caitlin Harley, ODOT Active Transportation Manager for updated bike related info in the Ohio Driver Manual (Digest of Motor Vehicle Laws);

local Roadway/Traffic Engineers Nancy Lyon Stadler and Andrés Saldaña for their helpful input on lane widths and safely maneuvering around cyclists; David W. Haug, CSP, ASP, Transportation Safety Director for sharing his safety expertise; Julie Knabe, for her help with cases so I could also work on this book; fellow attorney Sean Allan for insurance law input; Mark Davis, Doctor of Optometry, member of Institute of Functional Medicine/candidate for certification, and fellow cyclist, for sharing nutritional information;[VI] local cyclist/hero Michael Matlock for sharing his courageous story of fending off a dog attack while riding; KLF Office Manager Michele Hohm for her support throughout the creation of *Cycling Rights'* second edition; Paralegal Lisa Duchnowski for her valuable suggestions; Chuck Smith and Tricia Kovacs of Ohio Bicycle Federation (OBF);[VII] Sharon Montgomery for sharing her knowledge and personal experiences; the Ohio to Erie Trail team; and Rob Thompson, Attorney at Law for his thorough and always insightful input.

Ken Knabe
Lakewood, Ohio
November 30, 2023

All profits from the sale of this book are donated to Bike Cleveland, and other bike organizations, groups, and shops.
　　As it becomes available, information and updates regarding legislation, cycling laws, and more can be found at: https://klfohio.com/the-cycling-rights-book/

I.　https://www.parkermulhollandllc.com/

II.　https://www.keithberr.com/

III. https://www.bikecleveland.org/about/staff-board/

IV. https://www.amazon.com/dp/0998220434/

V. mjmclaughlin5@gmail.com

VI. https://www.europtical.net/

VII. http://www.ohiobike.org/

CONTENTS

01

....

LEGAL BIKE PRACTICE

IN THIS INITIAL CHAPTER, I share a bit more about myself as both a cyclist and an attorney. If you'd prefer to immediately start learning more about your cycling rights, skip ahead to Chapter Three.

Cycling is a major part of my life due to the benefits (see Chapter Two) and the camaraderie offered by riding the open road. I've ridden many century rides, have cycled toward a cure for cancer with Velosano,[1] and traversed the 326-mile Ohio to Erie Trail (OTET) in 2018 and 2022.[2] I'm on my road bike on Strava several times a week in decent weather, and during winter I ride my Wahoo indoor Kickr trainer.[3] I have a road bike, a gravel bike, and a trusty commuter.

I support fellow cyclists beyond representing them when they are injured in a bike crash. I served on Vision Zero Cleveland's Maintenance and Vehicle Fleet Sub-committee.

Vision Zero is safety legislation with the goal to "eliminate serious injuries and deaths from crashes on Cleveland roads".[4]

In 2021 Knabe Law Firm was awarded the **Bicycle Friendly Business 2021-2025 Silver designation** by the **League of American Bicyclists**.[5] This award recognizes KLF as a business offering "encouragement, education, and resources to help commuters, both in (its) staff and in (its) surrounding communities, bike safely and confidently from day one." KLF is one of only two Ohio law firms to receive this designation.

I am honored to have received Bike Cleveland's[6] **Guardian of Sustainable Transportation Award** for supporting local advocacy. I also sponsor Bike Cleveland's annual "Fundo".

I'm a Board Member of the **Ohio Bicycle Federation (OBF)**[7] and the **Ohio to Erie Trail (OTET)**.[8]

Finally, I've been a trial attorney for 40 years specializing in representing the injured. Professional ratings include **2023 Highest Legal Ability & Ethical Standards** and **2023 Ohio "Super Lawyer"**. I'm also an avid cyclist. This legal and cycling combination helps me to always protect cyclists from the ground, up!

My professional calling is representing—with dedication and compassion—fellow cyclists who are severely injured or worse in avoidable crashes caused by unsafe or distracted drivers. Knabe Law Firm is the only firm in Northern Ohio specifically geared to bike safety and serving cyclists injured in bike accidents.

02

....

BIKE BENEFITS

Can Cycling Save the World?!

BIKES ARE GOOD FOR OUR HEALTH

NO SURPRISE to learn that bikes are straight up good for **us**! This chapter discusses why bikes are good for the environment, good for our wallets, and good for where we live. An exceptionally well-controlled study tracking 263,450 people over five years found that those who biked or walked to work had a 41% lower risk of dying from all causes of death than those who drove or took public transport.[9] The longer the distance traveled, the greater the benefit. Best of all, a body in motion tends to stay in motion.

Mental acuity improves with cycling! Our brains work faster, and better thanks to fresh neurotransmitters and brain cells produced by cycling, which make the brain better at functioning, growing, and even repairing itself.[10]

If you haven't been on a bike in a while, start slowly, keep it realistic, and soon you'll be reaping the benefits.

BIKES ARE GOOD FOR AIR & WATER

Shorter Trips, Higher Emissions

"It's just a quick trip" is a common mindset when using a motor vehicle for those short rides to work or the nearest food market. However, at a trip's start the cold engine causes a motor vehicle to emit higher rates of carbon dioxide (CO_2) and volatile organic compounds (VOCs). And once back home with the engine turned off, "hot soak" occurs when evaporation causes even more VOCs to be released. Unfortunately, these factors add up to more emissions per mile than on longer trips.[11]

Even a small switch from motor vehicles to bikes can make an enormous difference to climate change! With modest decreases in motor vehicle usage, six to fourteen million tons of CO_2 would be kept out of the atmosphere. Another great reason to hop onto a bike for those shorter journeys rather than into a motor vehicle.[12]

With transportation the largest sector of carbon emissions in the U.S., the idea of "tackling climate change from the street up" by reducing motor vehicle emissions continues to gain traction, and the fact is, we have known for decades how important bikes can be.[13] Greenhouse gas emissions in the U.S. jumped 6.2% in the coronavirus pandemic's second year as more drivers got back on the roads in 2021 and usage of electricity generated by coal also increased. The U.S.

transportation sector, generating nearly a third of net U.S. emissions, had the biggest spike–10 %–just a year after emissions declined by 15% due to much quieter roadways. And for the first time since 2014 the electric power sector experienced a 6.6% emission increase due to higher natural gas prices leading to coal generation.

Paris Climate Agreement

The Paris Climate Agreement has the goal of capping the mean global temperature at below 2 degrees Celsius/3.6 degrees Fahrenheit over pre-industrial levels, hoping for an increase of no more than 1.5 degrees Celsius/27 degrees Fahrenheit. Ultimately the aim is carbon neutrality, a condition of net-zero CO_2 emissions.[14]

Research findings by the Rhodium Group include that while under the Paris Climate Agreement the Biden administration set a 2030 target for the U.S. to reduce emissions by at least 50% under 2005 levels, 2021 saw total U.S. greenhouse gas emission levels even **more** off the mark than those of 2020.[15]

State of the Air 2021

The American Lung Association released its annual "State of the Air" report for 2021 with a focus on soot (particle pollution) and smog (ozone). Diesel emissions, wood burning equipment, wildfires, and power plants using coal to generate electricity all create particle pollution. These threats to air quality can enter the lungs and bloodstream and cause serious respiratory and other cardiopulmonary health conditions.

The report includes Cleveland's mixed rankings for both particle pollution and ozone. Ozone–partly created when sunlight and heat cause chemical reactions between nitrous oxide and other VOCs (aka hydrocarbons) emitted by motor vehicles–got a failing grade despite fewer days with unhealthy air quality, and the city ranked 31st most polluted for ozone in the U.S. As for particle pollution, Metro Cleveland experienced an increase in unhealthy air days including daily spiking. Particle pollution throughout the year matched 2020 levels, landing the city at 14th for most polluted nationwide.

Most would agree that we all have the right to breathe healthy air. Climate change makes air quality worse and more challenging to clean up. Across the nation, 135 million people–over four in 10–are at risk from air pollution. And there is racial disparity concerning clean air; counties with unhealthy air were found more likely to be populated by people of color than white people. They also have a three times higher chance of residing in counties with failing air quality grades.[16]

More Bikes, Cleaner Lake

Beyond air, people often don't realize the impact motor vehicles have on our water. Given our mostly flat topography (making it easier to ride around without hills) on the shores of Lake Erie, places like Cleveland stand to win big if we can get more people on bikes. Motor vehicles using oil, grease, rubber, coolants, and chemicals will always deposit them on our roadways to be washed down the drain each time it rains. It has been shown that more bikes and fewer motor vehicles naturally reduce all these things. But when you go a step further and start designing Complete and Green Streets for multimodal use and integrate smart design features such as bioswales (linear ditches with vegetation which collect, filter, and convey stormwater), planted medians, and more permeable materials where possible, a lot of this pollution can be captured before it makes it to the lake, while making our streetscapes nicer, more inviting places.

BIKES ARE GOOD FOR LAND USE, TOURISM & REAL ESTATE

Beyond a healthier natural environment, there are real economic benefits to more bikes on the road and the associated infrastructure improvements in full swing across the nation. You can benefit from living in a bike-friendly location even if you don't own a bike!

Bikes Boost Property Values

Proximity to quality bicycle infrastructure such as protected bike lanes and trails frequently increases property values. In 2021 researchers at Arizona State University found that in Tempe, greater bicycle infrastructure density has a positive effect on residential real estate price and could ultimately mean higher revenue from property taxes.[17]

Famously in 2015, property values of homes adjacent to the 8.1-mile Indianapolis Cultural Trail yielded a $1.01 billion increase in value. In spring 2021, slightly closer to home, the Cincinnati Riding or Walking Network (CROWN)–to include 54 communities–finalized plans for another leg of bike trail that will be part of "a truly connected system of trails" around the city. Regarding those property values? With an ultimate total length of more than four times that of the Indianapolis Cultural Trail . . . you do the math.[18]

Touring by Bike

The term "bicycle tourism" is one we're hearing a lot more. The U.S. Bicycle Route System (USBRS) more than doubled in recent years and eventually will be nationwide, like its European analogs. And legislators are getting more protective of the financial gains generated by cyclists for their states. Montana, for example, benefits greatly from bike tourism, gaining close to $400 million annually. State legislators ultimately, and unanimously rejected the Senate Bill 363 amendment for a "bike tourist" tax of $25 per rider[19] after receiving hundreds of protest letters from bicycle advocates.

From large cities to villages, local economies and smaller businesses are also enjoying growth thanks to bike tourism. On Chicago's south side a former heavy metal dump was transformed into the 300-acre Big Marsh Park, opening in 2016 and offering bike tracks and jumps, and paths for birding enthusiasts. In 2021, the largest natural site in Chicago's Park District added more paved trails and the Ford Calumet Environmental Center. The themes of bikes and nature are celebrated annually at the "Birds, Bikes, and Beats" event.[20]

Locations in remote areas are benefiting from bicycle tourism as well. In Minnesota, land formerly used and left damaged by mining and timber industries is offering fresh challenges and adventure to cyclists, including mountain bikers. Their tourism dollars are both boosting the economies in smaller towns and encouraging the entrepreneurial minded to start new businesses. And this more organic, environmentally friendly use of the land is giving ecosystems a chance to heal and return to native habitats.[21]

Here in Ohio, according to a user survey, 90,000 visitors spend $13 million on goods and services related to the trails in the Miami Valley. It makes sense. It has been shown that people on bikes spend more dollars on average than their motor vehicle-driving counterparts. So, if you see people riding around your business district, it's probably a good sign that things are healthy!

Bike-ability Means Livability

When it comes to what makes a city or town "livable", ease of mobility and transportation choice are important, even political, factors. As a preface to the May 2022 primary election, Bike Cleveland in partnership with Clevelanders for Public Transit provided a questionnaire to all County Council and County Executive candidates covering issues around mobility and active transportation so constituents would know where the candidates stood regarding varied aspects of walking/biking such as air quality, infrastructure, personal health, safety, oil dependence, and economics.[22]

If you're an elected official or a city planner/engineer concerned with population decline, continuing to develop better bike and pedestrian infrastructure, and demonstrating commitment to this generation by meeting their transportation preferences is necessary if you want your community to grow and thrive.

The Bottom Line

The verdict is in. Bikes are good! Bikes are healthy and fun; they promote clean air and water and help make our cities less congested and safer. Bikes save us money, and if we let them, they might just help us to save the world. While that is happening, and while you're actively participating in the solution, make sure you **know your cycling rights** and make sure you **cycle right**!

03

·····················

CYCLIST RIGHTS ON THE ROAD

A BIKE IS A VEHICLE!

BICYCLES AND E-BIKES as defined in the Ohio Revised Code (ORC) are legal road "vehicles" in Ohio.[23 & 24] Thus, cyclists have an **absolute legal right to ride on the road in Ohio** except on divided, controlled access freeways.[25 & 26 & 27]

Cycling on the road is perfectly legal—except on divided, controlled access freeways like this one!

Cyclists Can't Be Forced to Ride on Sidewalks

Since Ohio law gives us the right to ride on the road, it also provides that cyclists cannot be restricted to riding on a sidewalk.[28] In fact, many local ordinances make it illegal to ride on a sidewalk, especially in a business district!

Sidewalks are frequently pockmarked, uneven, too close for a backing motor vehicle driver to see a cyclist, and littered, often containing gravel, glass, and dangerous sewers. Cyclists can be a hazard to pedestrians including slower walkers and parents pushing baby strollers. Although it is legal for cyclists to ride on sidewalks absent a local ordinance prohibiting it, sidewalks are generally not a good alternative to roadways.

Some cities, such as Columbus, allow children under the age of 10 to ride on sidewalks, but make it illegal for everyone else.[29] Cincinnati allows minors under the age of 15 to ride on sidewalks under certain circumstances.[30] The National Highway Transportation Safety Administration (NHTSA) agrees, stating in its "Bicycle Safety" publication that children under 10 are safer when cycling away from traffic because young children can't always make safe decisions when riding on the road unsupervised.[31]

Summary: It is legal to ride on a sidewalk if not prohibited by a local ordinance, yet municipalities can't force you to ride on them.[32] Be aware of possible sidewalk restrictions in local ordinances.

Please note: Per the ORC, even when sidewalk riding is allowed cyclists must yield to pedestrians, who legally have the right of way (ROW) on sidewalks.[33] Many municipalities, such as Cleveland, require an audible signal from a cyclist passing a pedestrian.[34]

Cyclists Cannot Be Required to Ride on the All Purpose Trail

Beyond traditional sidewalks, cyclists also can't be confined to riding on the "all purpose" trails in the Metroparks or elsewhere.[35] So, when driving a motor vehicle please keep in mind that the cyclists you see riding their bikes on the road in the Metroparks (for example) are doing so legally. Remember—the trail is not a "bike trail". It's an **all purpose** trail for walkers, hikers, leashed dogs, and bikes. Valley Parkway is a road and bikes are legal on it! It's a park, not a freeway; motorists don't own Valley Parkway!

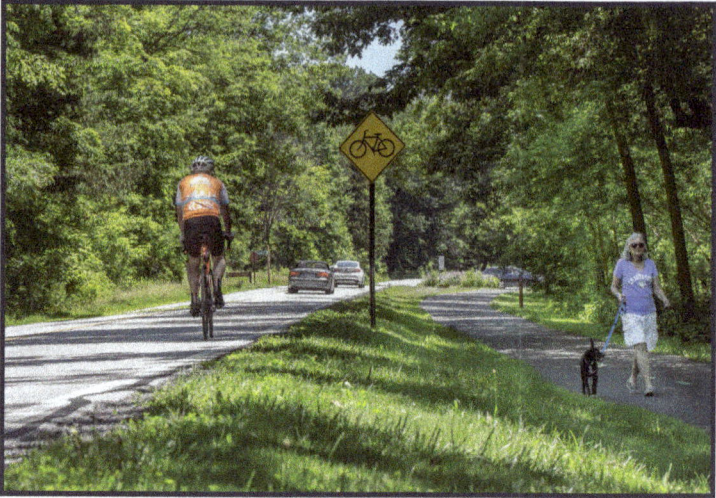

Cyclists have a legal right to ride on the
road including in the Metroparks

Can we ride two abreast?

Cyclists can ride two abreast on the road (unless riding on a path or part of a road reserved for the exclusive use of bicycles, in which case we may ride more than two abreast).[36] A very small minority of local ordinances still on the books prohibit riding two abreast.

Gates Mills, Ohio: Single File Ordinance

Local authorities can regulate bike operation independently to a degree, but no local ordinance can be fundamentally inconsistent with the ORC.[37] This means Ohio statutes generally take precedence over local ordinances which can supplement but not conflict with the ORC. This author's opinion is that single file statutes are invalid as they are fundamentally inconsistent with the ORC allowing two abreast. Conversely, a local ordinance providing **broader** cyclist rights that conflict with the ORC would also be invalid, as illustrated in *Kane v. City of Dayton* in Chapter 13.

Protecting Ohio Cyclists

Ohio has made progress regarding laws that protect us as cyclists.

Three-Foot Passing Law: Ohio's statewide three-foot minimum safe distance passing requirement. Drivers of motor vehicles must allow at least three feet between their vehicle and a cyclist when passing. This law became effective March 21, 2017.[38] Again, check your local ordinances for variations. For example—Cleveland has a six-foot passing ordinance for commercial trucks.[39]

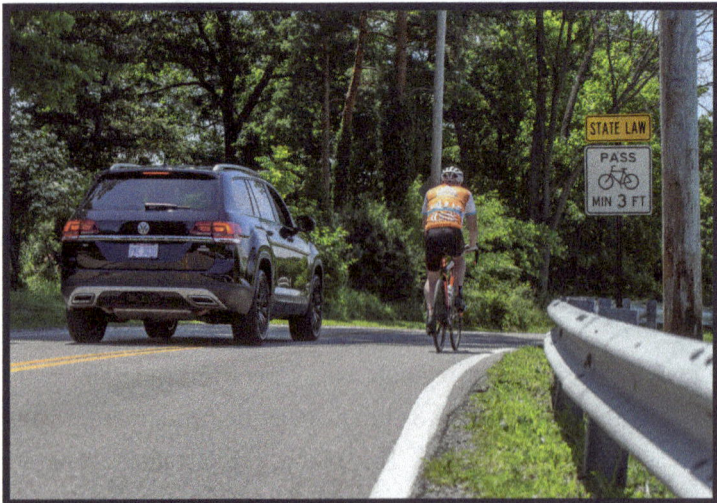

A vehicle safely passing a cyclist with three feet of clearance

One very important—and common—reason that we cyclists require a three feet or greater buffer between ourselves, and motor vehicles is that at times, we might need to ride farther to the left to avoid a hazard.

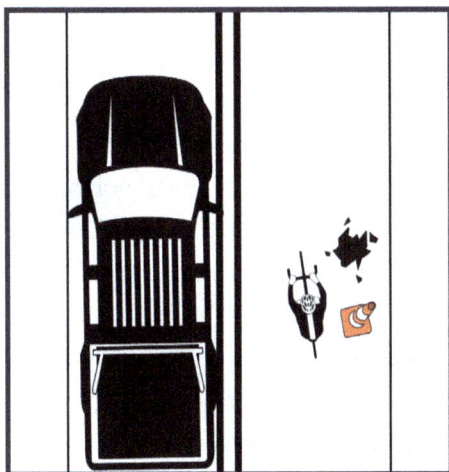

Dead Red Exception: Ohio's "dead red" exception permits a cyclist at a red light to stop, then safely enter the intersection on "dead red" which occurs **only** when a red light malfunctions/doesn't trip to green when failing to detect a bicycle's presence (many intersections only detect motor vehicles). This law became effective March 21, 2017.[40] The cyclist must make sure it is safe to go, since the cyclist won't have the right of way because the oncoming traffic light will still be green! This is not a law that allows cyclists to proceed through red lights unimpeded. Don't become a "dead" red statistic by misinterpreting this law!

Distracted Driving—Secondary Offense

Ohio's "secondary offense" distracted driving legislation, Ohio Revised Code §4511.991, became effective in October 2018 and was updated on April 4, 2023. "Distracted driving" is broadly defined as: *Engaging in any activity that is not necessary to the operation of a vehicle and impairs, or reasonably would be expected to impair, the ability of the operator to drive the vehicle safely.* If law enforcement believes that a motorist is distracted while committing a moving violation, and that the distraction is a contributing factor to the moving violation, the motorist is subject to an additional fine.[41]

This law made distracted driving a secondary offense, not a primary offense, meaning that a police officer could not pull a motorist over for distracted driving independently of another primary violation (such as speeding or failing to obey a traffic control device).

Driving while Texting—Primary Offense

I have great news! Ohio's "Driving while Texting" law, Ohio Revised Code §4511.204[42] became effective April 4, 2023. This statute makes holding cell phones and other electronic wireless communications devices while driving a **primary** traffic offense for all drivers. Law enforcement can now pull over and cite a texting driver without the driver committing another primary traffic offense, such as running a red light. There are over 10 exceptions, however, including hands-free use and a motorist using their phone when stopped at a red light, swiping to answer a call, and holding the phone to their ear during a call. Hands-free and emergency calls are always permitted.

Intersections

Ohio still needs to improve and clarify the law concerning the rights of cyclists crossing at intersections, giving them the same rights as pedestrians.

Punishment vs. Deterrent

The issue of punishment for motorists who catastrophically injure cyclists—especially hit-and-run drivers—is important, but so is the issue of justice for the cyclist. A deterrent doesn't help the victim, who always needs justice! In fact, the Ohio Bicycle Federation is working on a "Traffic Victim Support Act", legislation to hopefully achieve justice for vulnerable road users seriously injured or killed by unsafe drivers. Many states have vulnerable road user legislation and Ohio has begun patterning some of its own legislation on these existing laws.

BTW: Cyclists Also Pay for Roads!

Some motorists think they should have priority over cyclists on our roads because they "pay" for them through registration, taxes on gas, and licensing fees, and therefore "own" the road. This, however, is a misconception. While it is true that motorists pay tolls, gas tax, and registration fees (collectively "user fees"), these fees make up only 55% of Ohio's road budget.[43] The rest is comprised of general funds that come primarily from property tax and sales tax paid by people whether they drive a motor vehicle or not. If motorists were to bear the full brunt of the cost of our roads, the gas tax would need to be raised by over 75% to $0.50/gallon. In 2019—during which there was a 28-cent tax per gallon of gas—Ohio lawmakers began contemplating raising the gas tax to provide at least part of the $1 billion needed for all road and bridge repair.[44] The fuel tax ultimately was raised in 2019 in Ohio—38.5 cents for gas and 47 cents for diesel, with hybrid vehicle drivers paying an annual $100 flat fee and electric car drivers, $200 annually. According to the County Engineers Association of Ohio Executive Director Dean Ringle, "The gas tax helped but it didn't solve all the needs." Upwards of $4 million is still needed to "(get) our roads and bridges up to snuff. The needs we have are maintenance and replacement."[45]

Adding insult to injury, people generally ride on local streets which are primarily paid for with local property taxes and other sources of general revenue. Moreover, the reason roads are so expensive is that they are costly to maintain due to motor vehicles damaging them in a way that bicycles simply do not. To wit, a two-hundred-pound bicyclist with a fifty-pound bike will impose approximately **1/65,000**[th] the roadway damage of a four-thousand-pound motor vehicle![46] And once you start factoring in external costs of driving such as air and water pollution, it ends up costing society $0.29/mile to drive a motor vehicle, while a person on a bike generates an external cost of less than a penny a mile.

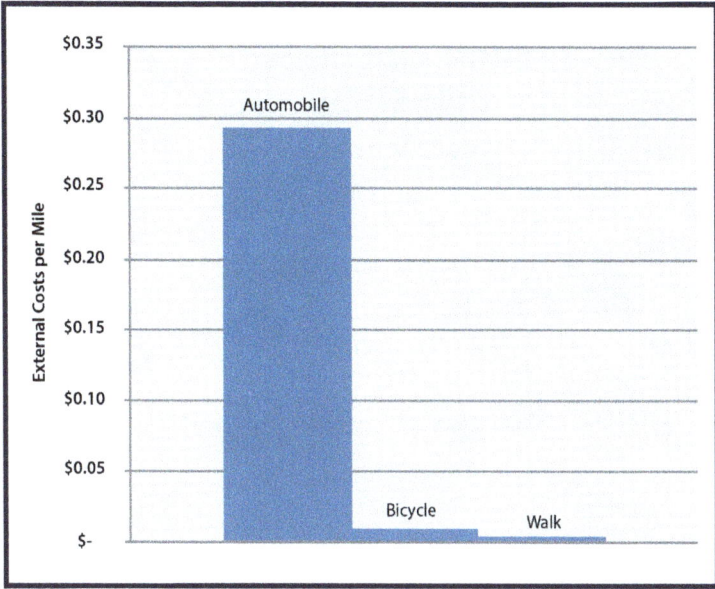

Source: U.S. PIRG Education Fund

Ultimately, the misconception is not only wrong, but reversed! People who bike, instead of driving, pay a much bigger share through their general fund contributions than motorists do through their user fee contributions; plus, a heavy majority of cyclists also own and drive motor vehicles, so they pay those fees as well, but on balance create far less damage and subsequent cost.[47] Cyclists not only belong on the roads, they cover their costs, something motorists have never been asked to do. And yet, as discussed in Carlton Reid's *Roads Were Not Built for Cars*,[48] our modern roadways were initially paved due to a bicycle boom in the early 1900s before motor vehicles had become available.

Truly, knowing this, motorists should be more than happy to follow the law, and share the road.

04

·············

CYCLIST RESPONSIBILITIES ON THE ROAD

A BIKE IS A VEHICLE WITH THE RIGHT TO RIDE ON THE ROAD

AS STATED IN CHAPTER THREE, a bike is a vehicle. Adult cyclists have an **absolute legal right to ride on the road** except on divided, controlled access freeways. [49 & 50 & 51] Bikes don't **block** traffic, they **are** traffic. Cyclists are not **in** the way of motorists, they are **on** their **own** way!

Vehicular Cycling

Originally coined by advocate and author, the late John Forester[52] in his 1976 book Effective Cycling,[53] "vehicular cycling" means (to this author) **riding our bikes on the road similarly to the way we drive our motor vehicles**, following the applicable traffic laws. John Forester deserves major credit for helping to define bicycles as vehicles with road rights. However, unlike some strict vehicular cycling proponents, this author believes in dedicated bike infrastructure including protected bike lanes, bike boxes, bicycle-specific signals, and other bike-specific road safety measures.

Finally, ride like your name and phone number are on your shirt or jersey and your reputation is at stake. This might temper some overreaction to aggressive motorist behavior.

Where do we ride on the road?

Some motorists, some police, and even some courts are of the erroneous belief that cyclists must ride as far to the right **as possible**. This is simply not true.

Ohio law provides that we must ride as near to the right side of the roadway as is "**practicable**" i.e., basically reasonable.[54] Riding to the right side is not required if it is unsafe. Many valid reasons exist for not staying at the road's right side include avoiding fixed or moving objects—such as parked or moving vehicles—and hazardous surfaces.

Also, if the lane is too narrow for a motor vehicle to safely pass a cyclist, the cyclist can take the full (whole) lane, and the motorist **must** wait for an opportunity to safely pass the cyclist (or group of cyclists).[55]

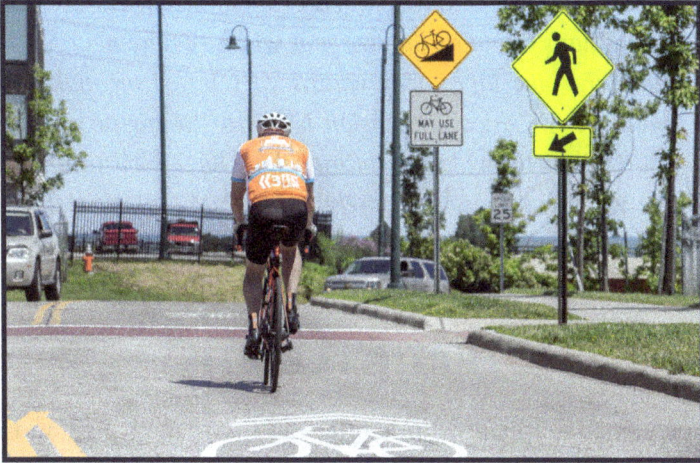

Ken taking the full lane

A cyclist can take the lane when the lane is too narrow for a motor vehicle to safely pass the cyclist. Exactly what does it mean? Many local authorities have signs saying "Cyclist (bike symbol) can take the full lane", which is great for cyclists and motorists having clarity; no measurements or guesses needed! I asked Cleveland-based Road Engineer, Nancy Lyon Stadler that question and this is her edited answer:

> "The standard width for a motor vehicle travel lane is 12 feet wide and can often be 10 feet wide in urban areas. These widths are insufficient to allow safe use by both motor vehicles and bicyclists without motor vehicles either crossing the roadway center line on a two-lane road or moving into the adjacent travel lane on a multilane road to safely pass a bicyclist. In Ohio, State law requires motor vehicles to allow a minimum of three feet clearance when passing a bicyclist. Bicycles safely travel along a curbed roadway at a distance of at least one-to-two feet from the

curb if the area is free of debris or other obstacles. These dimensions establish the five-foot width requirement for standard bike lanes. Car widths vary based on make/ model, etc. Critical dimension is mirror-to-mirror since that is likely the widest part (and what I have felt brushing me when cars pass too closely). On-street parking stalls are typically eight feet wide so that is a fairly reasonable assumption for car width with some clearance buffer."

THAT'S 13 FEET!

Nancy is a tri athlete who is often on the road cycling and is always seeking greater prevention and safety.

Local Roadway/Traffic Engineer Andrés Saldaña, E.I. agrees with Lyon Stadler's remarks:

"Lane widths vary in different locations but given the dimensions of a vehicle usually there will not be enough width for a vehicle to maneuver around the cyclist without crossing the center line."

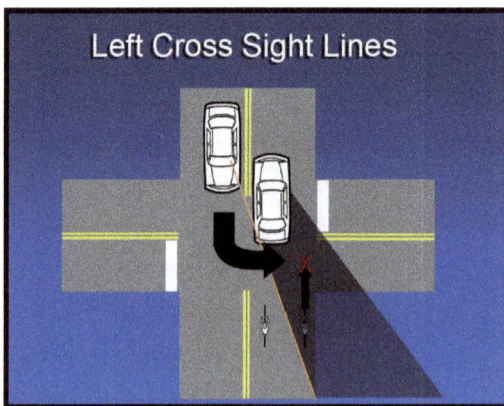

Sight Line advantages of taking the full lane
Source: BikeWalk NC

26

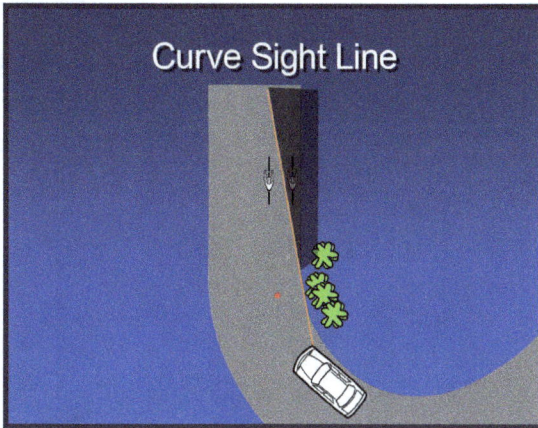

Curve Sight Line

Andrés' work as a traffic engineer is guided by his goal of always providing maximum safety for vulnerable road users like cyclists and pedestrians. Andres was hit on his bike by a car in the Metroparks, so he knows how it feels to be on the receiving end of a preventable crash!

Traffic Control Devices

Ohio cyclists are presently bound by the same laws as motorists, including stopping at red lights and stop signs.[56 & 57 & 58 & 59] Other states have more liberal laws concerning cyclist duties at these traffic control devices (see Chapter Seven) but at the time of writing, Ohio does not, barring the "Dead Red" exception. (See Ohio's "Dead Red" exception discussed in Chapter Three.)

Cleveland's first cyclist-specific traffic light (pictured here) is installed downtown with individual green/yellow/red lights in the shape of bicycles that follow the usual pattern for safer navigation of one of Cleveland's busy intersections along one of its priority bicycle corridors.

Cleveland's first bike signal downtown on the
Veterans Memorial (Detroit-Superior) Bridge

Cyclist compliance with traffic control devices goes way up when bike-specific infrastructure such as bike signals is present. When Chicago added a protected lane and bike-specific traffic signals to Dearborn Street, stoplight compliance of bicycles quickly rose from 31 to 81 percent. If you build it, they will comply.[60]

Hand Signals

Predictability is an important factor for cyclist safety. Whenever practical, a cyclist should try to avoid sudden, erratic movements or unnecessarily excessive weaving. Cyclists should try to announce their turns and stops with State-mandated hand signals[61] which I demonstrate here, and which don't have to be held continuously,[62] aren't necessary in turn lanes, and don't need to be given if they will interfere with the safe operation of the bike, e.g., if the rider is uncomfortable taking a hand off the handlebars.

Turning left: Left hand and arm extended horizontally

Turning right: Left hand and arm extended upward
(the "old school" right turn signal)

OR Turning right: right hand and arm extended horizontally
(the "modern" right turn signal)

*NOTE: Although both are legal, in modern times the "old school
right" (pictured on the previous page) may be confusing to younger
motorists, so I recommend using the "modern" version (also pictured)

Stopping, or decreasing speed:
Right hand and arm extended downward

Bike Lights

The ORC mandates that our bikes have specific, activated front white lights and red rear lights at **night (sunset to sunrise).**[63] No legal requirement exists in Ohio to have these activated lights on during the **day,** unless visibility (i.e., how far you can see ahead of you) is less than 1,000 feet due to atmospheric conditions (e.g., fog) or when windshield wiper use is necessary on motor vehicles (e.g., rain). In addition to a rear light, the ORC also requires you have a red rear reflector unless your light can perform this function as well.[64]

Cyclists should try to be prepared with these lights in case they end up riding at dusk or dawn, or during rainy or foggy periods with low visibility. Slower flashing lights have been found to be more accepted by motorists than those flashing faster. **And,** when riding in periods of dimmer light, wearing non-mandatory reflective garments and/or attached reflective strips that will bounce light back toward motorists with headlights on can additionally alert them to your presence on the road.

Some cyclists choose to activate daytime running lights to increase visibility: how visible you are to motorists and other forms of traffic around you. Even if a motorist is initially aware of you, by the time they're much closer you've somewhat blended into the surrounding scenery. That said, daytime lights are a personal choice, not a legal requirement. As previously mentioned, the 2020 pandemic created somewhat of a bicycle boom of new riders, and I'm still seeing many cyclists riding on the streets without lights on at sundown! All riders, experienced or new, should be aware that **Ohio law requires bike lights at night**.

Helmets

As of June 2020, no federal law exists making bike helmets a requirement. Ohio law doesn't require adults to wear bike helmets, but at the time of writing **24 cities** in Ohio require them for minors (including Lakewood), and if you live Shaker Heights, a local law requires them for adults.[65] My take on the subject? I prefer to wear a helmet. I see the foam cracked on the inside of many helmets due to bike crashes. I would rather crack my helmet than my head!

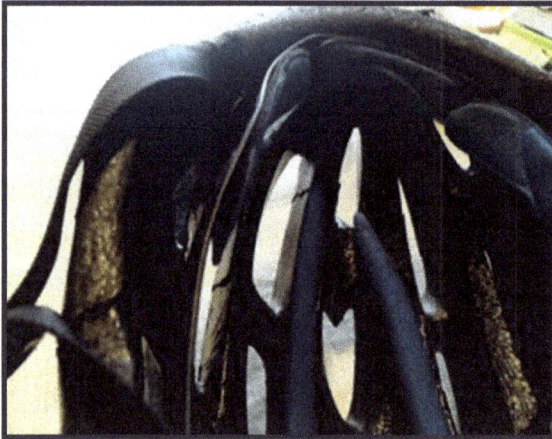

Bike helmet with cracked interior

The efficacy of wearing a bike helmet is the subject of much debate and is generally a **personal**, not legal, choice for adults. Some cyclists don't want them, others can't afford them. Because of equity concerns around affordability, we don't want the State or local authorities (defined as every county, municipal, and other local board or body having authority to adopt police regulations under the constitution and laws of this state) mandating helmets, and one argument is that it could result in potential police targeting of low-income people for unrelated reasons.

Nevertheless, with head injuries causing approximately three-quarters of cyclist fatalities and one review finding that with helmet use, the risk of brain or head injury in any kind of bike crash dropped by approximately two-thirds,[66] wearing a helmet is something to consider. Bike club etiquette generally calls for wearing one, and many local group rides will not allow you to join the ride without one.

A May 2021 report by the U.S. Consumer Product Safety Commission (CPSC) focuses on a helmet's power to reduce risk of traumatic brain injury (TBI) and milder forms of head injury.[67] From 2009 through 2018 approximately 597,000 cyclists were treated for TBI in the emergency departments of U.S. hospitals. While no helmet at the time of writing can completely prevent the possibility of a TBI, the CPSC advises consumers, including cyclists and those engaged in other sports, to wear a helmet the correct way:

- Be sure helmet fits according to manufacturer instructions; no tipped up helmets, or tipped to one side.

- Replace helmet if it has been worn in a crash— damage can be invisible; be sure to bring helmet to your bike attorney so it can be photographed/ documented!

- Replace helmet if straps are worn out or another part is missing.

- Be sure helmet has an internal label confirming it meets the federal safety standard of CPSC.

Serious, long-lasting head/brain injuries can and do occur. Global advancements in helmet technology include Sweden's "Multi-Directional Impact Protection System" aka "MIPS", first available in 2010 and Oregon's "WaveCel" released in 2019 claim to reduce head injuries and increase favorable outcomes. Fluid Inside™ is a newer Canadian technology which manages linear and rotational impact via a matrix of fluid "Pods" inside the helmet that mimic cerebrospinal fluid (CSF). At the university's dedicated helmet lab, students and faculty at Virginia Tech conduct unbiased helmet testing that is "much more rigorous than U.S. consumer standards".[68] Extensive research includes both road and gravel bike helmets.

How much better or effective these newer helmet technologies are, only time will tell, and it's important to remember that helmets are not a cure-all. Concussions are common in bike crashes, with some injured cyclists suffering ongoing, debilitating symptoms. It's a good idea to familiarize yourself with the symptoms of concussion and post-concussion syndrome[69] which many cyclists develop after a head impact, even when wearing a helmet.

Other options include "smart" helmets on the market which have:

- Directional indicators: A great safety feature **in addition** to the State-mandated hand signals you're already using!

- Speakers: An alternate to headphones and/or for making calls; at the time of writing Ohio law does not prohibit this feature.

- Built-in lights: To make you more visible to other road users.

- Bluetooth: Handy for GPS, music/podcasts/ audiobooks; at the time of writing there is no restriction in Ohio law on helmets with this capability.

- SOS mode: Notifies emergency contact in the event of sudden jolt, followed by no movement of helmet; controlled by an app.

Visibility

No legal "visibility requirement" exists for cyclists in Ohio— what people wear when they ride is also a matter of **personal**, not legal, choice. As cyclists we do not want the government mandating the specifics of our cycling wardrobes. However, a practical non-legal suggestion for cyclists wanting to stay extra visible is to consider wearing clothing that stands out from the environment, such as bright and/or fluorescent clothing.

Reflective garments or strips can be especially effective on rotating parts of your bike and clothing, e.g., pedals, wheels, shorts, socks, and shoes.

One review of multiple studies found drivers consistently recognized fluorescent colors faster—and from a greater distance—than standard hues. This is due to fluorescent material reflecting non-visible ultraviolet light back in the visible spectrum, which makes it far better than conventional colors during the day. Fluorescent colors appear approximately 200 percent brighter.

Although no research supports a "best contrast" color, fluorescent orange can be a great choice because drivers typically associate it with caution, e.g., construction signs and highway safety. In addition, the color orange is rare in the natural environment.

A caveat: From sunset to sunrise, with no natural light for the fabric to reflect, fluorescents will not help keep you safer on your bike! Neither motor vehicle headlights nor streetlamps emit UV light. On night rides your fluorescent yellow jacket will be no brighter than anything else you might wear.[70] Instead, you should wear reflective clothing at night for better visibility.

Also! Pedaling movement aids visibility, especially on roadways where a lot of coasting is possible. Continuing to pedal helps to catch the eyes of motorists around you. At an intersection, it can also signal your intention of going straight rather than making a turn.

Since it's not legally mandated in Ohio, no defense exists for any cyclist's personal decision or financial inability to purchase or wear a particular type of clothing. In other words, if a careless motorist hits a cyclist, the motorist has no legal defense that the cyclist "could have or should have been wearing brighter or fluorescent clothing or gear". That would be akin to arguing that a motor vehicle that was smashed into from behind should've been painted in bright or neon colors!

Traffic Tickets

When cycling, **we can be ticketed, but no BMV points can be assessed on our driver licenses—unless it's a driving under the influence (DUI) situation!**[71] If you drink above the legal limit and then ride, you'll risk getting a DUI with all the points and suspensions applicable to a driver of a motor vehicle **and** the added penalty of a non-expungable criminal offense. By the way, drinking does not make you a better rider!

Never waive a bike traffic ticket unless you are sure that **no points** will be assessed on your driver license. Believe me, cyclists often get BMV points because some courts, some prosecutors, and even some police don't know that points **cannot** be assessed for a bike traffic ticket that isn't a DUI.

Knabe Law Firm has a supply of laminated bike cards with a **"Cyclist's Arsenal"** that includes the Ohio statute providing that cyclists cannot receive BMV points for traffic offenses except DUI, and other current Ohio bike laws all cyclists should have at their fingertips while out on the road. The flip side will help you remember the important steps to take in the event of a crash, should one unfortunately occur. Please contact Knabe Law Firm to request a complementary card be mailed to you.

05

· · · · · · · · · · · · ·

ROAD SITUATIONS & ISSUES ENCOUNTERED BY CYCLISTS

THIS CHAPTER OFFERS an overview of road situations we cyclists encounter—from legally navigating turns, intersections, sidewalks, and other bike infrastructure—to handling the sticky situations that sometimes come up on our roadways.

How do I make a left turn in Ohio?

§4511.36(A)(2)[72] states:

At any intersection where traffic is permitted to move in both directions on each roadway entering the intersection, an approach for a left turn shall be made in that portion of the right half of the roadway nearest the center line thereof and by passing to the right of such center line where it enters

KNABE LAW FIRM L.P.A.

the intersection and after entering the intersection the left turn shall be made so as to leave the intersection to the right of the center line of the roadway being entered. Whenever practicable the left turn shall be made in that portion of the intersection to the left of the center of the intersection.

This is the same basic process used when turning a motor vehicle at an intersection in which traffic is traveling in both directions. As cyclists we need to make the left turn from the lane nearest the center line. Once we begin the left turn, we obviously must stay to the right of the center line of the road we're entering. Before turning (unless already in a designated turning lane) remember to try using a left-hand turn hand signal at some point if you can do so without jeopardizing your safety.

When cycling we should try to prepare for making left turns by gradually moving into the lane closest to the center line as we approach the intersection. If you feel comfortable and safe doing so, a hand signal may help you to merge left, to get into position to make the left-hand turn. The sooner we anticipate the merge, the easier it is to maneuver to the left lane (or, if there is only one lane in that direction, the left portion of the lane we are in) from which we'll be turning.[73] I use a Garmin Varia back light that signals my GPS if any motor vehicles are behind me when I try to merge.

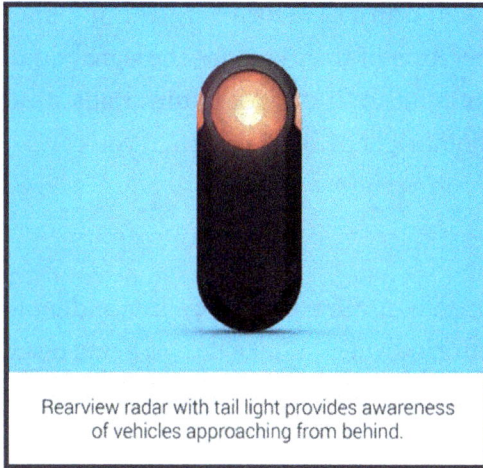

Rearview radar with tail light provides awareness
of vehicles approaching from behind.

Source: Garmin Ltd.

The left turn hand signal doesn't have to be held continuously. If stopped to turn left, it's a good idea to simply point left before you turn, if you can.

How do I make a right turn in Ohio?

§4511.36(A)(1)[74] states:

Approach for a right turn and a right turn shall be made as close as practicable to the right-hand curb or edge of the roadway.

At an intersection, to make a lawful right turn in Ohio, we should ride our bikes to the right of the lane as close as is "practicable" to the curb on the right side, or to the edge of the road. This statute is vague, in that it refers to the curb **or** the edge. Try to make a right turn from the safest turning point on the road lane to the right. Cyclists turning right should try to give a right-hand turn hand signal before or during the right turn, unless in a right turn only lane or it interferes with the safe operation of their bicycle. The signal doesn't have to be held continuously. If stopped to turn right, it's a good idea to simply point right before you turn, if you can.

Bike Boxes

To help mitigate turning for both cyclists and motorists, bike infrastructure known as a "bike box" is being installed in cities across the U.S. According to the National Association of City Transportation Officials (NACTO).[75]

A bike box is "a designated area at the head of a traffic lane at a signalized intersection that provides bicyclists with a safe and visible way to get ahead of queuing traffic during the red signal phase".

A "two-stage bike box" is a little different and helps people on bikes make left turns without the drama of making an unnerving left merge in busy traffic—a "normal left". Essentially, a two-stage bike box creates a space for cyclists to get across an intersection, stop, position themselves facing left, wait for the light to change, and then proceed. This sequence looks a lot like a pedestrian crossing the street, waiting for the next light to change then crossing again, only it's all done on the road within the right of way.

With bike boxes, groups of cyclists can move through intersections and crosswalks more quickly, minimizing wait time for motor vehicles, public transit vehicles, and pedestrians. As of this writing, two-stage bike boxes can be found in Cleveland at both the eastern and western ends of the Veterans Memorial (Detroit-Superior) Bridge.

Downtown Cleveland bike box

The City of Lakewood added bike boxes to Lake Avenue in fall 2020 and provides a helpful infographic (under Lake Avenue Striping) on its website.[76]

Regarding Bikes and Intersections...

NACTO published its *Urban Bikeway Design Guide* back in 2011.[77] Since then, the mileage of protected bike lanes across North America has increased over 600%! While this statistic is impressive it has also highlighted the need for better intersection design. Of all urban cycling fatalities in 2017, 43% of them happened at intersections.[78] NACTO's report released in May 2019 and titled *Don't Give Up at the Intersection* includes information illustrating how design factors such as lane width and turning radii can affect motorist decisions. The wider the lane and the larger the turn radius, the easier it is for a driver of a motor vehicle to make a fast "sweeping" turn, which makes intersections more dangerous for people on bikes and on foot.[79] Generally, if motorists are given too much space, they will use it to speed without even thinking about it. Therefore, good street design is critical.

What is a "sharrow"?
Do roads or lanes with sharrows differ from designated bike lanes?

A sharrow is an image of two chevrons above a bicycle logo, painted onto the street. Though like a bike lane symbol to the untrained eye, sharrows are typically **used in shared-use travel lanes** (think regular streets) **of 35 mph or less** and **do not set aside specific space for bicycles**.

Sharrows are eleven feet from the curb in areas with on-street parking, and four feet from the curb where there's no parking. Theoretically a sharrow has several functions, potentially helping cyclists to position correctly in the lane, to avoid getting "doored" while cycling past a parked motor vehicle, and to be regarded as legit by other road users. This author agrees with Bike Cleveland's position that a street with a sharrow painted on it doesn't comprise a complete bicycle facility when used alone. They are best used in conjunction with other road treatments such as "Bicycles May Use Full Lane" (BMUFL) signage, when the speed limit is **preferably at or below 25 mph**, and only on streets where a better type of facility or road treatment isn't feasible.

Sharrow painted on shared-use travel lane

PeopleForBikes' senior director for infrastructure, Dave Snyder shares how he's become disillusioned about sharrows since his earlier days as executive director of the San Francisco Bicycle Coalition. Although a 2010 report showed that sharrows led to some positive behavioral changes, and the city still uses them, officials don't expect them to do much to increase safe cycling on the roadways. Snyder also believes that merely slapping painted sharrows on streets can allow officials to take credit for something that does almost nothing for cyclist safety. He reiterates the need for separate bike paths, protected bike lanes on busier roads, and speed reduction on shared use lanes.[80]

Bike Lanes

Striped bike lanes—perhaps the most common form of easily recognizable bicycle infrastructure—are usually two solid painted lines near the right edge of a street and include a bike lane symbol (a painted bicycle image accompanied by a solid arrow pointing in the direction of travel). You will find these all over the country, and for many bicycle advocates they constitute the minimum acceptable level of bike infrastructure.

Bike Lane—and Dooring Zone markings—in Lakewood, Ohio

Designated bike lanes are generally much preferred over shared use lanes marked with sharrows because they **reserve specific space for people to ride bikes**, whereas sharrows—without providing any separation, much less protection!—merely help people understand that bikes also may use regular travel lanes. At the time of writing Cleveland has three protected bike lanes: on the Veterans Memorial (Detroit-Superior) Bridge, on Payne Avenue starting at the bridge over I-90, and over the Fulton Avenue bridge. Bike Cleveland recognizes one other protected bike lane, an off-road trail in Opportunity Corridor, and continues advocating for many more.

Protected bike lane in Cleveland with bollards/delineators

A Cleveland municipal ordinance provides that cyclists have the right of way when riding in a designated bicycle lane. Motor vehicles shall not and cannot drive in any bike lane, or otherwise place a vehicle in a bike lane in a way that could impede bicycle traffic, including parking in one. Motorists may still **briefly** cross bike lanes to make turns, access parking, and to enter or exit the roadway, but these exceptions only apply when the bike lane is clear of any bike traffic.[81]

People's Streets Cleveland, a volunteer run grassroots initiative partnering with eight groups including AsiaTown Advisory Committee and Bike Cleveland, shares a vision of safer streets for all ages and modes of road users while connecting diverse neighborhoods, bringing together people who may not have interacted previously.

The initiative's streetscape enhancements to the Payne Avenue corridor include decorative, culturally themed painting on crosswalks and curb extensions on six streets between and including East 22nd and East 39th. As of this writing, temporary bike lanes with bollards are also on Payne Avenue across the I-90 bridge and eventually will be replaced when this section of roadway is reconstructed and repaved.

Did I mention that parking in bike lanes is not allowed in Cleveland? No vehicle, except for a bicycle, can stand or be parked in a bike lane.[82]

What about aggressive motorist behavior such as honking or yelling, or worse?

Many, if not most cyclists have been honked at by impatient motorists who likely think there's no rule against it, and who are upset with us for exercising our legal right to ride on the road. However, "unnecessary sounding of horns" **is** prohibited in Cleveland's municipal code.[83]

It's important to remember that most motorists are courteous and pass without incident, but any cyclist will tell you they routinely experience verbal hostility and even physical intimidation from drivers of motor vehicles unhappy with our presence. The animosity is lessening somewhat, but at the Firm we still see situations in which a motorist becomes unjustifiably annoyed with a cyclist and then:

- Drives past a cyclist and intentionally turns in front of them, causing the cyclist to either crash into the motor vehicle or veer in a direction that puts them in unnecessary danger.

- Drives past a cyclist, intentionally close.

- Stops motor vehicle, gets out, and verbally and/or physically assaults the cyclist.

Unofficial rule number one for us cyclists: As tough as it is when someone is yelling at us, the best practice for a cyclist is to resist joining the argument. This will only fuel the anger of a motorist and make you look bad. You also can't gauge a motorist's mental stability, whether they're driving while intoxicated, and even scarier, if they have a weapon on them or in their vehicle. The sooner you've both moved on, the safer you will be. Call the police!

06

GROUP
RIDING

VISIBILITY, PREDICTABILITY
AND DEPENDABILITY

GROUP RIDING! Camaraderie, drafting, greater distances, enjoyment, better visibility, and fun. Love it, avoid it? We all land somewhere in between but we almost all end up in a group ride of some sort.

Best to think about group riding safety **before** joining a group, especially since individual riders generally assume the risk of injury, even injuries caused by negligent fellow riders. In this all-new second edition chapter, I share both legal and practical knowledge focusing on our ultimate goal: riding safely.

Before I get started . . . **kudos to the ride leaders** who volunteer to guide and instruct groups, promoting safety and smooth riding!

BE PREPARED: Know the Ride Parameters

Each group ride has its own organic or written rules and etiquette. Most organized club ride rules are typically published on club websites. Do your homework beforehand. For other group rides, ask how the group generally rides, e.g., group size, distances, experience levels, pacelines, drop/no drop . . .

Clubs offer different ride levels—be sure to research all levels so you'll know where you'll best fit in. If you join a group in which you can't keep up, you slow the group down and diminish everybody's enjoyment. On the other hand, maybe you can push yourself to levels that you thought might be beyond your reach!

Pre-Ride Checklist:

- **Arrive on time!** Best practice is to arrive at least 20 minutes early and make sure you are ready to roll at the start time.

- **Maintenance:** Get your bike tuned by one of the many great Northeast Ohio bike shops before the ride. Always arrive at a ride with bike and equipment working well.

- **Bike check:** Air pressure, tire leaks, tire wear/bubbles, brakes . . . nothing worse than riding with someone who is always getting flats! When tightened properly, the quick release should leave a momentary imprint on your palm. Remember **ABC**: Check the **air** in your tires and make sure the thru-axle or quick release in the hub is tightened and secured; check the **brakes**; check the **chain** alignment in the chain rings and cassette.

- **Tire issues:** Always have a **tire lever**, an **extra tube that fits**, and a **tire canister inflater or pump** with you. Don't assume another rider will have items you can use. Even if you can't fix a flat, you should carry what you need to fix one.

- **Designate** a ride leader and get the leader's cell number.

- **Inform** the ride leader if you have any health concerns.

- **Inform** the ride leader and the other riders if you're leaving the ride early and where you will be leaving the ride.

- **Sign** registration waiver form, if applicable.

- **In Case of Emergency (ICE):** Be sure to have a **road ID** or other form of identification and include emergency contact info.

- **Hydration!** Be sure to bring enough water and electrolytes, and snacks for longer rides. This makes a huge difference! Pop an electrolyte tablet in your water bottle. Hydrate **before** you start. (See nutrition section later in chapter for more info.)

- **Helmets!** Make sure yours is up to date and has MIPS!

- **Other protective gear:** Gloves, eye protection, sunscreen.

- **Lights!** Front white and back red lights are legally required at night (dusk to dawn). **Little known fact:** these lights are also required in periods of low visibility, e.g., fog & rain—if motor vehicle headlights or windshield wipers are on, your lights must be on! So, it's a good idea to always have front white and back red lights on your bike, ready to use and activate at sundown or if your group ride gets delayed into dusk, or it starts to rain or get foggy (as often happens). It's frightening for me when I see a cyclist at night riding illegally with no lights, playing Russian Roulette with passing cars! When you see car lights on, your bike lights should be on.

- **Extra lights?** Consider an extra white light on the side of the fork and a red light on the side of the seat stay, for greater visibility from the side to oncoming motorists turning or entering an intersection. You can also use them if one of your front or back lights is not working.

- **Daytime running lights:** A personal, not legal, choice. Hopefully, they add more visibility! Due to intensity, some daytime running lights can hinder other cyclists riding or drafting directly behind you, so place your back light on a low setting unless you are riding alone. In that case, crank it up!

- **Know where you are going!** Some phones allow you to save routes in various apps like Strava. If you have an onboard GPS unit such as a Garmin or a Wahoo, you should be able to download the route for turn-by-turn directions. Download "Ride with GPS".

- An **onboard computer** like a Garmin or a Wahoo that tracks your speed is also extremely helpful in maintaining an even speed and teaching you what a certain speed "feels" like. Depending on the features you want, decent computers can be as inexpensive as $25 or as much as $500!

- **Cell phones:** Avoid talking on your cell phone while riding except in case of emergency.

- **The correct bike!** If you're going to ride a road bike, be familiar with—and comfortable with—riding "clipless" pedals (clipless actually means that your shoes clip into the pedals; clipless is older verbiage from when cyclists wore harnesses or cages called "clips").

- **Are e-bikes allowed?** If so, which classes? Most clubs only allow a Class 1 and prefer pedal assist mode only, not throttle. Typical bike club insurance does not cover Class 2 because it can operate totally under throttle mode; Class 3 can go up to 28 mph, so some clubs disallow them especially since the ride can end up on all purpose trails where Class 3 bikes are prohibited. (See Chapter 15: E-Bikes & Ohio Law.)

- **The pace:** What are the speed limit parameters, e.g., 12-15 mph, 15-18 mph, 18-20 mph, 20-23 mph? Are groups designated A,B,C, or D or by 1, 2, 3, or 4? Who is tracking and enforcing the speed limits? Normally, it's the ride leader or the **"sweeper"** or **"sweep"** (the designated last rider who monitors the group's riders).

- **Pusher:** Ride within the group-designated pace or join another group. Don't be a **"pusher"**: a cyclist who is too strong for the group and violates the agreed upon speed limit parameters, pushing the other riders out of their comfort zone. Conversely, don't be a **"poser"** and ride with a group in which you cannot keep up!

- **Wanderer:** Also, don't be a **"wanderer"**: ride predictably and straight; zigzagging all over the road leads to confusion with motorists as to your intentions.

- **Regroup and adjust:** For example, you're coming out of the Valley Parkway or the CVNP and into the city. The next thing you know, you're turning left on West 65th to get to Edgewater Park. West 65th north of Detroit Avenue has plenty of restaurants, bars, traffic, and on-street parking. You now have to adjust–slow down and pay very close attention to vehicle and pedestrian movement.

Nutrition & Hydration for Cyclists 101

- **Pre-ride**, it's a good idea, before even getting on the bike, to hydrate. Drink a bottle of water!

- According to my cycling buddy Dr. Mark Davis of Europtical, **hydration is the most important aspect of nutrition in cycling.** Once you are thirsty it's too late, drink soon and often. How much? Well, that depends on the ride, but plan on 16-20 ounces every hour and start drinking within 15 minutes to prevent dehydration, which potentially leads to muscle cramping. Continue to drink every 15-20 minutes.

- **If your ride is under an hour, plain water is adequate; over an hour, add electrolyte powder to both bottles.** There are a lot of companies making electrolyte products for athletes. Get one you like and check the sugars; try not to buy those with the highest sugar content. Look for products that have at least some magnesium, sodium, and some vitamins such as Bs and C (OSMO, Nuun Electrolyte Sport and Nuun Endurance—for a long ride—are good choices). Also, take along some instant glucose for if you start to bonk, anything like Stingers, Shot Blocks or Skratch.

- **How to tell if you or your buddy is bonking?** If they say something absurd. My friend Tim rode his first "Century" on the famous "Sunday in June" ride event put on by the Cleveland Touring Club. He is one of the most avid riders I know. Yet, nearing completion, Tim yelled "Look at the size of that bird!" My buddy Steve and I looked over to where he was pointing and saw a little sparrow! Or, as on my Ohio to Erie Trail ride, during day three from Columbus to Akron I was sitting on a boulder across from The Ohio & Erie Canal with my head down and an empty bottle next to me. I was bonked because I had gotten lost—adding 20 more miles to the ride—and did not fill up when I had the chance! Especially on an unsupported group ride such as this one on the OTET, never pass up a chance to fill up those water bottles! Thankfully, my buddy Mark (Looney, author of the Foreword) came along and saved me by having an extra full bottle of electrolyte charged water.

- **Post-ride**—especially if the ride is over an hour—**you have a nutrition replenishment window of 45-60 minutes.** Post-ride drinks with whey protein and branch chain amino acids are good choices and aid in recovery. If you experience night cramps, look into magnesium supplements or pickle juice in its raw or liquid form. Enjoy the ride so much more by staying hydrated!

Group Riding Formations, Pacelines, and Drafting

- **Determine the ride formation.** Is it a simple single line where the first rider leads until that lead rider tires and then the next rider takes over? Is it a two side-by-side casual ride where the lead two drop back when tired? Do the lead riders drop back after 30 seconds, 10 seconds? Is it a single or a double paceline? Is it a peloton?

- Is it a "**No Drop**" (**ND**) ride? Is it a "**You're On Your Own**" (**YOYO**) ride? If a rider cannot keep up and is unfamiliar with the route, a stronger rider should get that rider back to the start.

- **The unexpected.** If a mechanical (or some other) issue occurs, especially on an ND, the group should stop and pull off in a safe place clear of the road and intersections. If there is an accident with injuries, call 911 and remember that due to adrenaline, the injured party may not be the best judge of their condition.

- **Different pacelines exist.** Generally, the top three formations are various versions of the single or double rotating paceline or a peloton type. If unfamiliar or uncomfortable with drafting, avoid joining a paceline until you are comfortable.

- **Single and double pacelines revolve around the advantages of "drafting".** As noted in Chapter Seven, when another cyclist riding in front of you is blocking the wind, it takes you approximately 25-30% less effort/ energy to maintain a speed 20 mph or above. The leader who is "pulling" is taking the full force of the wind. This allows the rest of the group to use less energy yet match the leader's speed in their draft. Group riders take turns leading, allowing the entire group to maintain a greater speed for a longer distance than a solo rider could.

SINGLE/STRAIGHT PACELINE: This is the most used group paceline. In the single paceline, each cyclist takes turns leading. After a short time, the lead cyclist moves left and drops to the back of the group. This is also the preferred method when traffic is heavy.

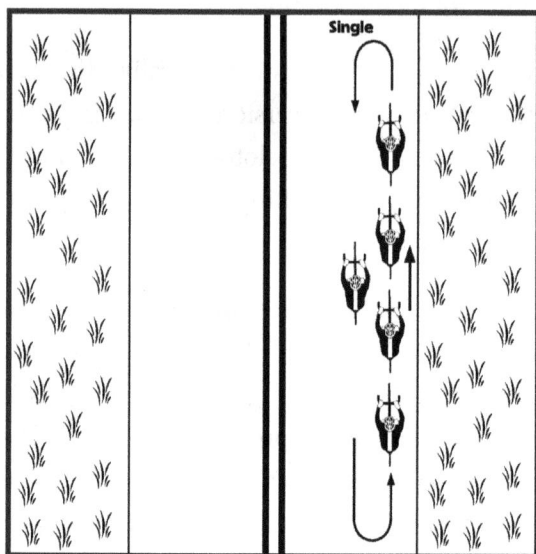

Do point out hazards: When you lead or **"pull"** the paceline, remember that nobody drafting behind you likely can see what you see—so, point out hazards. Each cyclist should then pass the hazard signal down the line. You **want** to be a **"pointer"** on any group ride—pointing out hazards, turns, direction you're heading—especially at intersections. Pointers communicate intentions to other riders and motorists!

Roadway hazards to watch for:

o Seasonal debris such as wet leaves, twigs, branches (often concealed by puddles).

o Slippery surfaces due to atmospheric moisture combining with grease/oil.

o Surface cracks running parallel to bike tires.

o Gravel.

o Cobblestone and brick roads.

o Bridges: expansion joints and grates can be slippery; consider walking your bike across a bridge and slow down, especially under wet conditions.

If you see a road hazard, try to skirt around it; avoid bunny-hopping over it, because your rear tire still might get caught in the hazard!

• **Avoid drifting**: When you move left to drop from the lead to the back, don't be a **"drifter"** (a cyclist who drifts left into oncoming vehicles)! And don't drift left in front of a passing car.

• **Leader moving to the back.** When a leader's time is up, they should flick their elbow out to the side before moving to the left and to the back, and only move left to the back if there is no passing car.

- **Braking.** The leader and group riders should try to keep pedaling and avoid slamming on the brakes! Use your pedals to increase or decrease speed or maybe a light feather on the brakes when drafting. Always signal or yell when breaking or stopping suddenly. If the lead rider misses a turn, the rider should not stop suddenly and risk causing an accordion-type crash. Rather, the lead rider should signal "stopping" and come to a gradual stop before turning the group around to safely make the missed turn.

- **Pulling.** The leader should not "pull" too long—let others take turn leading the paceline.

- **No gaps!** If you are drafting behind the leader or another rider, don't create gaps.

- **No overlaps!** Avoid overlapping your front wheel with the back wheel of the rider in front of you.

- **Hincapie Rule.** Follow the Hincapie Rule I learned when I took a bike skills class in Asheville. Cyclists should **never cross** the double yellow line. Respect the yellow line because danger exists on the other side!

- **Out of the saddle.** When you are in a group ride drafting and you stand out of the saddle, you actually fall back a bit! Warn the rider behind you with a flick that you are getting out of the saddle.

DOUBLE/CIRCULAR PACELINE: Now we are getting into more skilled riding! This explanation is difficult unless you have done it. Studying the following diagram will make this explanation a lot easier to follow.

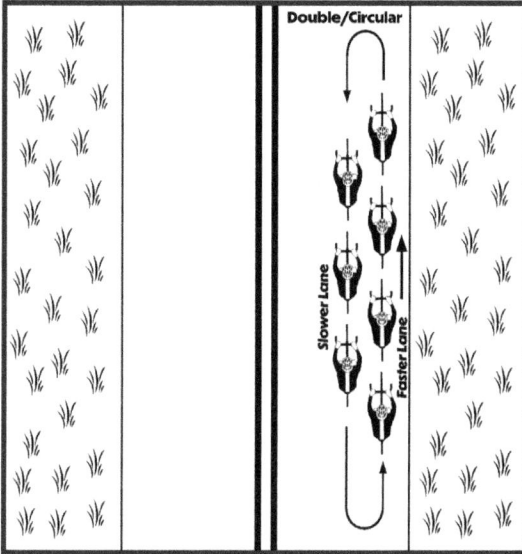

In a double paceline, two lines of cyclists exist; the right curb line and the left inner line. The slower left inner line receives the overtaking cyclist from the curb line to the inner line once the leader of the inner lane "clears" the cyclist. The riders in the inner lane eventually fall back and move to the right to the curb line and repeat the circular rotation.

- **Double paceline** takes experience, confidence, familiarity, and ability; avoid gaps and surging; riders must have a computer to keep track of speed limit; and moving too far left, near or past a double yellow, is a **no**.

- **No overlaps.** As with single pacelines, avoid overlapping your front wheel with the back wheel of the rider in front of you.

- **Fear the mental drift!** When in a double paceline group ride, unfocused mental drifting can lead to crashes. Drifting occurs when a cyclist is tired or lulled into a false sense of security relying on the rider in front, or by pleasant conditions causing the cyclist to go into their own mentally unfocused zone. Protect yourself by maintaining a **healthy fear of drifting**. Start your rides well-rested; make conversation with your fellow riders; follow routes with variety and interest, e.g., with hills and/or more traffic; stay in the present moment and pay attention to the sounds/smells/sights around you; take the lead occasionally; and, of course, **keep your guard up** and **always stay alert**!

- **Get off the road!** When stopping for a break or repairs, move completely off the road.

- **Regrouping!** Always leave and stay off the roadway when it's time to regroup.

- **Passing:** Normally, you always try to pass fellow cyclists on the left. In a double paceline, you are actually passing the slower rider paceline on the right, but everyone is aware of that situation.

- **Fear the Clear!** Avoid saying "clear" because what is clear for **you** may not be for the **cyclists behind you**; a better practice is to say "rolling" or "going". The rider(s) behind you can then determine if it is clear for them.

Remember you must ride relaxed and look ahead—not down at your wheel!

- **Slower and Faster Groups:** "You gotta keep 'em **separated**" (!) This line from "Come Out and Play" by The Offspring kind of says it all. If you have a group, you have a group for a reason. If a faster group passes yours, don't try to ride with them at the top of your limits because you will slow them down and mess up the cadence of that group's ride. This can be especially dangerous on downhills when two different levels of group riders meet and merge! Don't mix!

- **Pelaton:** Group riders in a pack riding side by side in no particular order. Don't ride more than two abreast and look to previous single and double paceline advice.

THE RIDE! Where do we ride on the road?

- **Ride right:** To the **right** of the road as is **"practicable"** (not "possible")—this means you don't need to ride on the right edge of the road; usually you want to ride about where the right rear tire of a car would be riding, so that your presence is more obvious to motor vehicles. Even when riding to the right, you can obviously avoid a pothole/parked car/debris (see Chapter Three).

- **Take full lane:** When a lane is **too narrow** for a motorist to safely pass a group of cyclists, cyclists can **take the full lane** (see Chapter Four).

- **Berm:** Best practice is to ride on the road and avoid the berm/shoulder which may or may not be considered part of the roadway. However, if you do ride on the berm because you feel it's safer due to congested or high-speed traffic, make sure you are riding in the direction of traffic and when leaving the berm and entering the road, do so **carefully** because you may not have the right of way (ROW) until you get back on the road.

- **Sidewalks:** Ohio law allows you to ride on the sidewalk, but many local ordinances prohibit it; using the sidewalk on a group ride only occurs in rare circumstances. (A big problem with sidewalk riding occurs when you enter an intersection; most local laws consider you to be a pedestrian at that point. Better to be on the road!)

- **Two abreast:** Under Ohio law we can ride **two** (not three or four or five) abreast; keep your ride group on the smaller side, preferably five to ten riders, and no more than fifteen as a courtesy to other drivers. When the group gets to be over 10, implement "platooning", i.e., breaking the larger group into two groups. This usually happens organically, BTW. Note: Some local authorities still prohibit riding two abreast! (See Chapter Three.)

- **Passing and crossing!** A cyclist's right side is a blind spot; always try to pass another cyclist on the left (except in pacelines).

- **Eye contact:** Try to make **eye contact** with motorists at intersections and enter just as motor vehicles do.

- **Railroad tracks:** Always cross railroad tracks at right angles.

- **Motor vehicle passing cyclists:** On a blind curve, the last rider in line can take the whole lane and essentially block a motor vehicle from passing the group; if not possible or preferable, all riders should be alerted to a passing motor vehicle.

- **Stay alert and aware!** Don't wear headphones or earbuds while riding.

- **Riding on the All Purpose Trail (APT):** A lot of bike clubs or group rides end up on the APT–remember, Class 3 e-bikes are not allowed to ride on them, therefore they are excluded from most club rides; consider the APT a two-lane highway and try not to cross over the imaginary double yellow; don't stop on the APT to talk or make an adjustment or repair, get off it!

- **Red lights:** Several states, such as Idaho, allow cyclists to treat red lights as stop signs and stop signs as yield signs. This is **not** the case in Ohio, but the Ohio Dead Red law is the exception. See Chapter Three.

- **Stop signs:** (Always **stop**! It's the law.) That said, the best practice may be to stop as a group and proceed as a group. While it's **not 100% legal** for a group of cyclists to move through stop signs together, it is a courtesy to motorists (see Chapter Four).

- **Use State-mandated hand signals** for left and right turns and slowing or stopping (see Chapter Four). Good idea to simply point in the direction you are turning if you can keep your balance.

- **Don't move left unless it's safe!** Use a Garmin Varia back light to warn you of oncoming vehicles approaching from behind you as you merge left to turn.

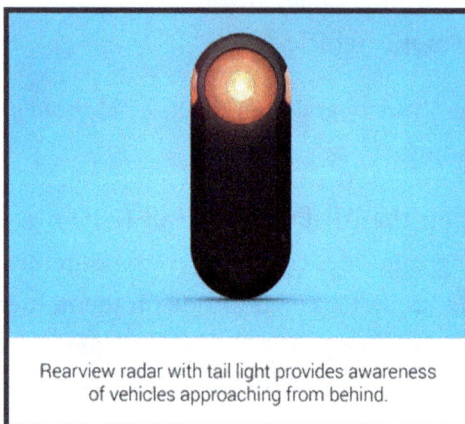

Rearview radar with tail light provides awareness of vehicles approaching from behind.

Source: Garmin Ltd.

Or, have a rear-view mirror. Also, remember the Hincapie Rule—never cross on a double yellow.

- **Mixed traffic?** A group of cyclists is safest and most efficient when the entire group moves together. While everyone needs to have situational awareness, the leader needs to be aware of the entire group having time to make it through each road situation! For example, the leader needs to know if there's enough space in traffic for the whole group to turn left at a stop sign or green light. Riders at the back of the group shouldn't have to choose between keeping up (and possibly being in danger) and being dropped. If one, or half of you make the turn or light, wait off to the side of the road for the others!

- **Take it easy:** Leaders should go easy out of corners and intersections.

- **Filtering?** As covered in Chapter Seven, cyclists will often **"filter"** up the side of a line of traffic waiting at a red light and place themselves at the front of the line. Absent a bike lane, cyclists are generally supposed to wait in line like motorists and avoid filtering. However, practical reasons exist as to why a cyclist chooses to filter. They may believe they will be more visible up front, and thus safer, in mixed traffic often containing much larger vehicles. In addition, when positioned first in the queue and most easily anticipating when the light will change, a cyclist may be able to clear the intersection more quickly, which may be safer for them given the high crash rates at those locations.

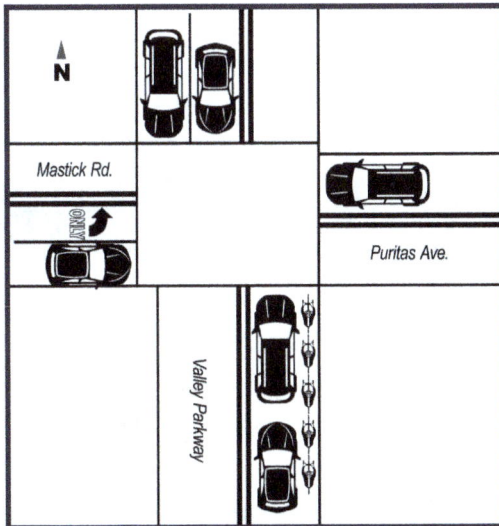

Filtering

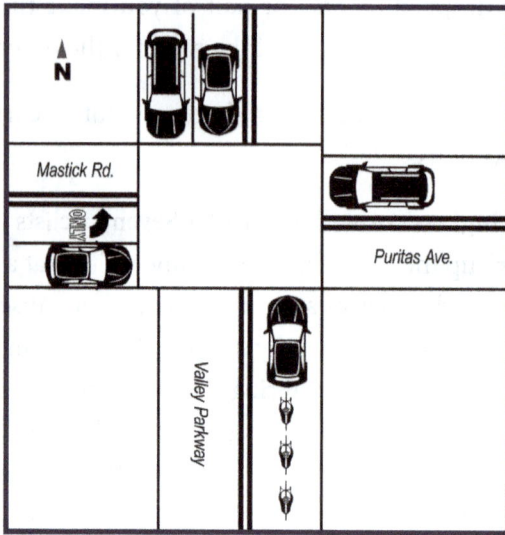

Not Filtering

Personally, I generally prefer not to filter. I also prefer to **take the lane**, so the oncoming left-turning vehicles see me!

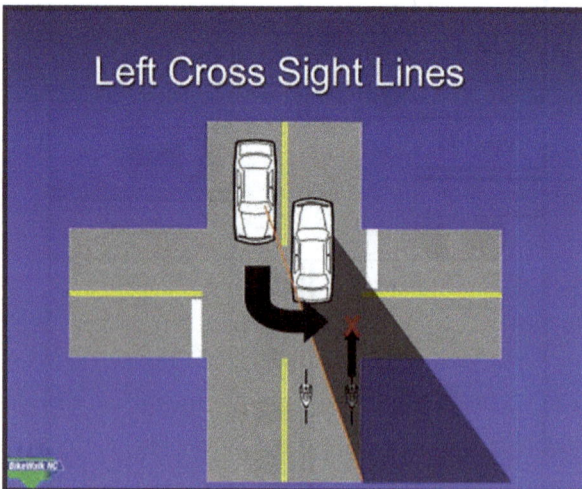

Source: BikeWalk NC

- **Don't Pass hand signals.** A **"don't pass"** hand signal to the motorist behind you can be helpful when taking the lane. Providing you can safely ride one-handed, holding the left hand high with fingers spread and palm facing a motorist behind, you can let them know your intention is for the motorist not to pass the group at that point (usually a blind curve). Also, the last rider can raise their left hand up and down from the shoulder telling the oncoming driver not to pass because a car is coming the opposite way.

- **Hand & verbal signals for leader/all.** For group safety, communication is key! **Communicate your intentions with other road users!** In addition to the State-mandated signals for turns, stopping and slowing illustrated in Chapter Four, group leaders and riders could use the following extra hand signals.

- **Pointing:** Point at ground to warn of debris or rough patches. The signal should be passed down the line by each rider so other riders can avoid it. If you can't point in time, just yell "Hole left!"

- **Motioning:** Hand behind the lower back, then point with motion left or right, to warn that you are moving left or right to avoid oncoming road hazards (e.g., parked motor vehicles, joggers, debris).

- **Waving:** Wave lateral arm up and down to indicate slowing.

- **Stopping:** Raise arm up or down behind the back to indicate stopping or slowing. If an abrupt stop is needed, **shout it out!**

LEAVING THE GROUP

- **Communicating:** If you are leaving the group for any reason, before the ride finishes, you should verbally tell the ride leader or sweep and remind the riders in your group that you are dropping or leaving the ride.

- **It's okay to drop or leave a ride, just communicate!** Many reasons exist for dropping or leaving. The pace could be too hot, maybe you've had enough, or maybe your house comes along earlier in the ride or is in a different direction. The point is to let the group know you are dropping or leaving the ride. Make sure you leave the ride safely by falling to the back of the group well before turning or stopping.

ROAD CONDITIONS

Wind

- **Wind direction** dictates the angle of how a group should draft. If the wind is coming **straight on**, you should be behind the back wheel of the rider in front of you:

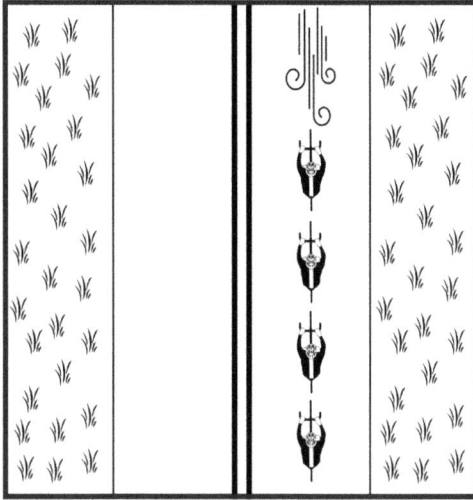

- If the wind is coming **from the right**, riders in the group should angle slightly to the left:

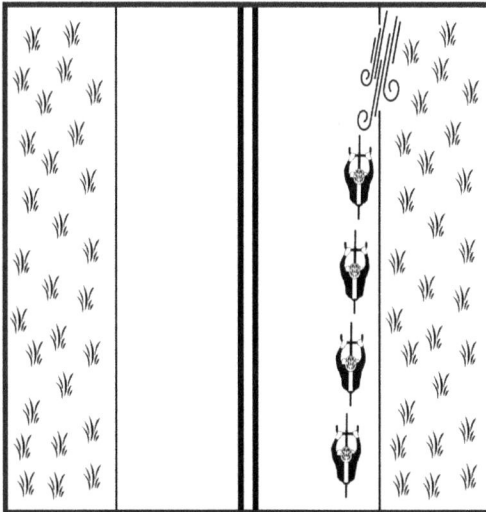

- And if the wind is coming **from the left**, riders should angle slightly to the right:

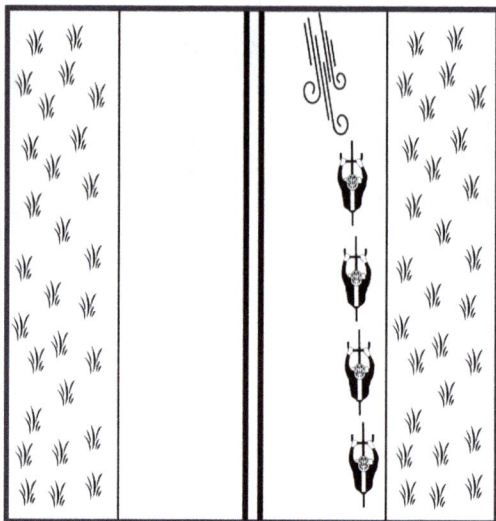

Sun

Sun glare can be a blinder and when a motorist is not seeing what's on the road, it can be lethal to cyclists. **Your shadow tells you where your blind spot exists for oncoming motorists,** as depicted in the following illustrations:

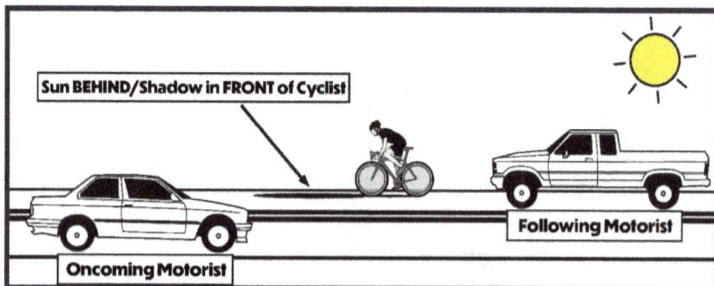

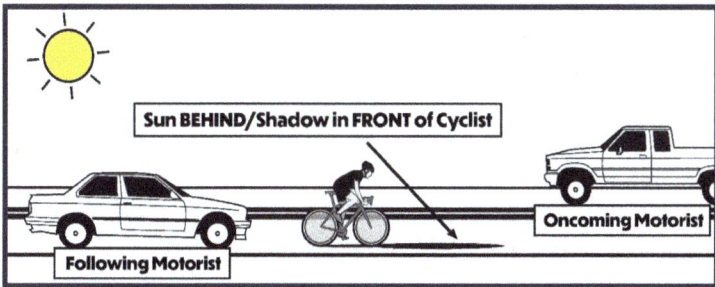

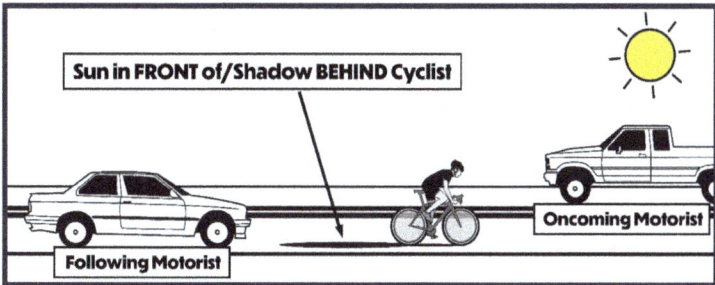

- Bottom line: Be aware of your blind spot.

- If the sun is glaring, take a different route.

- Use your lights, front and back on the highest setting.

- Wear polarized sunglasses.

Hills: Leading a Group in Hilly Terrain

Hills can offer cyclists the biggest challenges, the biggest thrills, and the biggest dangers! Downhill is where most group crashes happen, and steep downhills can be especially dangerous.

- **Climbing!** For the sake of everyone in the group, the leader should naturally go slower and steady on the uphill, leaving gaps between riders; keep a steady pace over the top, and **pedal** downhill, trying not to surge ahead of the group. When climbing, give extra room to riders in front of you; keep your head up and watch for stopped motor vehicles in your lane, animals, or a motor vehicle that passes you or suddenly stops in front of you while your head is down and you're pumping the pedals. Keep your speed low but steady and under control!

- **Descending!** The downhill is the great equalizer because everybody's fast on the downhill and weight is more important than skill. The heavier rider will beat the lighter rider down the hill every time if neither is pedaling!

- **Spacing:** Allow enough space between your bike and the bike in front of you.

- **Warning when passing:** Try not to pass on the descent, but if you do, pass on the left and give ample warning.

- **No sudden braking or stopping:** Sudden stops are a bad idea when a group of cyclists is descending a hill; don't stop or brake suddenly if you don't have to.

- **Moderating your speed:** Don't go over the speed limit! Keep your downhill pace moderate.

- **No-fly zone:** Never fly down hills; stay in control, look ahead for objects, animals, and defects.

- **Prepare:** Remember the descent ends so be prepared to stop fully under control, or you will wind up in an intersection or in the woods heading for a Sonny Bono tree!

- **Downright dangerous:** Slowing down, especially suddenly on a downhill is **dangerous** and could cause a chain reaction—something you never want on a downhill (or anywhere else).

- **Racing and passing:** Don't race down the hill and past descending motor vehicles. Drivers may freak out, not know what to do and simply stop. There is huge danger to a cyclist riding fast behind a car stopping or slowing on a downhill. Avoid descending if you see motor vehicles in front of you also descending.

Leaving the Group on a Downhill

When leaving the group, get to the back of the group and let them know that you'll be turning off. This is especially important when going down a hill. Never lead the group or be in the middle of the group when you plan on stopping on a downhill to leave the group. Always fall to the rear and let the rest of the people know you will be turning off. Also, if you are heading straight and the group is turning, you can take the lead and tell the group that you will be going straight when the group turns behind you.

Finishing the ride: The ride leader should account for all the riders and if one is missing, investigate. Again, if you drop, inform the ride leader.

Dogs!

In June 2023 the United States Postal Service (USPS) released details regarding dog attacks on its employees in Cleveland. Of all U.S. cities, Cleveland is ranked fourth! And it's not much safer outside the city with Ohio landing in fifth place. Not only is this a scary statistic for those delivering our mail, but it also confirms that uncontrolled dogs are out there–and potentially hazardous to us cyclists, as well.[84]

- If a menacing dog comes at you, remember to stay the course–an abrupt change of lane could take you into oncoming traffic, and you don't want that! Opinions vary on whether you should try to out-cycle the dog or not, but you should obviously do everything you can to keep it from biting you or knocking you off your bike. If you are in a group ride, a group effort may be needed to chase the dog away! If you see a dog up ahead, let the group know– yell "dog up", "dog right", etc. Yell **loudly**!

- Also, the dog may come into your lane in front of you and a collision could occur in which you fall off your bike. So, anticipate this and do your best to react carefully to avoid hitting the menacing dog.

A few more tips:

- **Be on the lookout**—warn other cyclists.

- **Best defense:** Don't engage—cycle away quickly if you can!

- **Have attitude:** Big Dog Energy can intimidate/discourage aggressive dogs. Yelling in a dominant voice—"No!" or "Go home!" can be effective.

- **Bigger groups** of cyclists are more likely to scare off, and be better able to defend against, a canine attack.

- Sometimes a **squirt from your water bottle** is enough to deter an aggressive dog.

- **Pepper spray** can work **but** not all are created equal; milder sprays are made for deterring dogs; human-strength spray can also be used to get you safe, without harming a dog long-term. Spray types include cone (covers wider area) and stream, preferred (minimizes wind blowback). If riding alone, however, a cyclist can be an easier target and carrying pepper spray is something to seriously consider. Before heading out on your bike, make sure you can easily access the spray. If you don't have pepper spray, you can spray the dog with your water bottle or throw your water bottle at it.

- As shared by Silver Wheels Cycling Club, **keeping one foot unclipped** and free to kick an attacking dog is an option.

- If you or someone on a group ride is knocked down, bitten, or attacked by a dog and injury occurs, do everything you can to identify which residence the dog came from, who owns the dog, and the type/breed of dog. Take photos of everything! Ohio law puts absolute liability on the dog owner or someone harboring in those situations, absent teasing, tormenting, or trespassing. Call the police and the animal warden or the local county Board of Health so they can investigate, and identify and cite the responsible party.

And while nobody should want to harm an innocent animal, the Ohio Revised Code also details circumstances when it is legal to maim or kill a dog in self-defense without being subject to animal cruelty charges:

- (A) Subject to divisions (A)(2) and (3) of section 955.261 of the Revised Code, a dog that is **chasing** or **approaching in a menacing fashion** or **apparent attitude of attack**, that **attempts to bite** or **otherwise endanger**, or that **kills or injures** a person . . . **can be killed at the time of that chasing, threatening, harassment, approaching, attempt, killing, or injury.** If, in attempting to kill such a dog, a person wounds it, the person is **not liable to prosecution** under the penal laws that punish cruelty to animals.

The statute[85] also speaks to an owner's personal liability; under Ohio law, if a dog causes a cyclist injury, the dog owner is statutorily liable for the cyclist's injuries unless the cyclist is trespassing or teasing or tormenting the dog.

- **Warded off a dog attack while riding:**

Michael Matlock, aka "The Shield" stopped by my law office and shared how he recently warded off a dangerous dog attack while riding. An unleashed, hostile, unconfined Pit Bull bolted out of a home's front door and pursued Michael, exhibiting various attack postures. Michael used his bicycle as a protection shield, trapping the dog with shear downward force and lodging it between the bike's tires and sprocket. According to the police report the dog "posed danger with an intent to bite cyclist multiple times". Fortunately, Michael's quick thinking–not to mention **guts!**–allowed him to avoid a negative outcome.

Michael Matlock, aka "The Shield"

- **Unfortunate cyclist:** A cyclist was riding solo in 2022 in a rural area of Ohio when she had a flat tire. While walking to her car, she was attacked and nearly killed by no less than three vicious, unrestrained dogs. The cyclist lost a leg and had to learn how to walk again, with a prosthetic and the remaining leg still recovering from injuries. **Incredibly,** the owner of these menacing dogs was only charged with misdemeanors! Not only does this situation show a lack of criminal penalties for Ohio dog owners, but it also shows an indirect benefit of riding with a group. This is **not** to say I'm blaming the cyclist **in the least** for riding by herself.

These are dramatic cases and examples of what could happen if approached or attacked by an aggressive canine. My intention here is not to make you fearful, but mindful.

ALTERCATIONS! MINDING OUR MANNERS ON THE ROAD

Cyclist vs. Motorist

Conditions continue to improve for us cyclists on our roadways, yet some motorists still dislike us and aren't happy that we're "sharing the road". A way to prevent–or at least mitigate–negativity coming our way is to stay on the metaphorical high road and remain as calm and non-reactive as possible. Like it or not, we're representing the entire cycling community when group riding. And when cyclists are following the rules of the road and being predictable, crashes are greatly reduced.

That being said, altercations can and do occur amongst cyclists and motorists. First, know this: the only time you can hit someone or damage their property is when you are acting in self-defense from the other's physical attack. Even then, your defense cannot turn into offense once the threat is removed. If you start the fight and hit someone, that is an intentional act, and it usually means that no liability insurance such as homeowner insurance is going to cover you. Why? Because insurance does not cover intentional acts! This is public policy, because otherwise a person could insure themselves to hit or hurt someone!

So, even in a road rage incident, cyclists' actions/reactions such as throwing water bottles, coffee, or other objects at motorists, punching their cars, etc. are all off limits! Watch out for being drawn into an overly aggressive mentality when a group of cyclists is confronted by an irate, potentially dangerous motorist; things can get out of hand quickly in a group situation consisting of several cyclists vs. one driver behind a 2,000-pound potential killing machine. If you do react as above, you have now entered the realm of criminal damaging and possible assault, and that driver who is completely at fault and out of line now has something against you to tell the police! **Simply call the police.** Also, don't chase down a road-rager or abuser or attack them physically. You will then be the one going to jail–not them. This seems so basic and understandable, but in the heat of battle out on the road where life and death can occur, some of these decisions are not so easy. Best to think about them before they happen and monitor your expected reactions so if these heated situations do occur, you can **back off** and save yourself.

The movies and TV give people the false impression that getting into a fight is cool and punching someone in the face is just fighting. As a former prosecutor, boy do I know that's not true. One punch to the face usually results in an orbital fracture, a concussion (that's a brain injury!) and could even result in death. Now you have committed a felony and are going not to jail, but to prison. Hitting someone is a last resort and should only be done in self-defense. Stay cool, my cycling friends.

Cyclist vs. Cyclist

Hassles in group rides can occur between cyclists, e.g., e-bike vs. muscle-powered bike riders, sometimes leading to altercations. No matter what the bike type, all group riders should be viewed equally, and all riders should respect one another. A million reasons exist for someone choosing an e-bike, and all e-bike riders are in the fold.

Bike Crash during Group Ride

Admittedly this is a bummer topic and none of us cyclists want to think about it. It's our duty, however, when cycling solo or in a group, to have a plan for coping with a crash should one occur.

The first step to take in a group ride crash (or even just a mechanical failure) is for one of the riders to go to the end of the group and let oncoming traffic know there is a crash scene so they can safely navigate around it.

Then, as soon as possible, take the following actions:

- Call the police and **insist** on a report, **no matter what**; you need documentation! **Always** call the police, even if the motorist begs you not to and/or seems like a saint or even if the police try to talk you out of filing a report! If you don't, the lack of a record and documentation of the crash will cause you later suffering! Some police like to give careless motorists a break. **If possible, don't let them!** Always request that the officer cites the motorist for the appropriate traffic offense.

- **Call an ambulance** if there are visible injuries.

- Get the motorist's contact and insurance info, and names of all witnesses, or try to make sure the police or other witnesses or bystanders obtain this vital information.

- After a crash, try to be your own legal reporter and document in detail all you can see and recall until police arrive on the scene. At some point, if you can, take pictures of your bike, the motor vehicle that hit you, your wounds, and your ripped/damaged clothing. Don't let the at fault party move their motor vehicle **or** your bicycle before the police arrive. Look for a building security camera that may have recorded the crash. Be sure to keep all damaged property (without cleaning or repairing it) including, for example, the bike frame, ripped clothing and accessories, and make sure you check the inside and outside of your cracked helmet for signs of head impact that may not be remembered or apparent to you in the moments after a crash. These items can be **valuable pieces of evidence**. In the moments after being hit this can be particularly difficult, but if you're able, this is an important step. If you have a modern GPS-enabled bicycle computer such as a Garmin or a Wahoo, check the data for the actual speed and location of where the crash took place, and let your attorney know if you have ride footage from a GoPro-type camera. These cameras, along with non-mandated daytime lights, are a growing trend among cyclists as they take additional steps in an attempt to protect themselves. Tell your attorney if you are on Strava or MapMyRide or a similar ride app so your information can be downloaded. And as soon as you can, start keeping a daily journal of symptoms, treatments, days off work, etc. This documentation will give your attorney a detailed picture of the impact the careless driver is having on your life. Once you've started a treatment plan such as physical therapy, it's best to attend all sessions and leave no "gaps" in your treatment.

Saving a Life: Stopping the Bleed

The Akron Bike Club wisely addressed the issue of stopping a bleed on a ride. None of us want to think about any kind of severe bleeding injury from a bike crash but unfortunately, they happen. Essential for stopping a wound's bleeding is knowing how to place and tie a tourniquet. The Department of Homeland Security's Stop the Bleed document[86] outlines the steps of tourniquet tying:

• Expose the wound and apply firm, direct pressure using clean cloth, gauze, an elbow, hand, or knee–whatever slows or stops the hemorrhaging.

- If bleeding doesn't stop, place a tourniquet two-three inches from the wound, **between the wound and the heart**; do not place tourniquet over a joint.

- Manually tighten tourniquet as much as possible.

- Make a note of the time the tourniquet was applied for caregivers who will be treating the patient.

Ohio Bike Cases: Group Riding

In Chapter 13 I share details from a wide variety of bike related cases. Here I focus on those involving group riding.

Case type: CYCLIST VS CYCLIST—GROUP RIDING, PRIMARY ASSUMPTION OF THE RISK
Kalan v. Fox, **187 Ohio App. 3d 687, 2010-Ohio-2951, 933 N.E.2d 337, 2010 Ohio App. LEXIS 2448**

The law for group rides can be unfavorable regarding pursuing injury claims against fellow riders. Due to a legal doctrine called "primary assumption of the risk", to recover civil damages from a fellow rider who injures another on a group ride by conduct that is an actual or customary part of group cycling, the rider must be more than careless or negligent; the rider must have acted recklessly or intentionally! Negligence standard applies when injury is occasioned by conduct that is not an actual or customary part of the sport, i.e., conduct causing unforeseeable risks.

Case type: CYCLIST VS CYCLIST—GROUP RIDING, PRIMARY ASSUMPTION OF THE RISK
Weglicki v. Rachitskiy, 2022-Ohio-254,
183 N.E.3d 1260, 2022 Ohio App. LEXIS 221, 2022 WL
278174 (Jan. 31, 2022)
Weglicki v. Rachitskiy, Geauga C.P. No. 2021-G-0010
(April 15, 2021)

Some recent Court action emanates out of Geauga County from a cyclist-on-cyclist crash during an organized group ride. A cyclist allegedly stopped to turn on a downhill so he could prematurely leave the group for home, allegedly without warning. Another cyclist riding behind him ran into him and sustained injuries. That cyclist sued the stopped cyclist who said he gave an arm signal. The Trial Court found that negligence is an insufficient basis to sue a fellow cyclist on a group ride by this conduct. The injured cyclist could only recover if the stopping cyclist was reckless. Since no evidence existed to establish recklessness on behalf of the cyclist being sued, the Trial Court dismissed the case.

The Court of Appeals reversed the Trial Court's dismissal of the case because the Trial Court failed to consider the injured cyclist's bicycle crash expert's opinions. Weglicki, supra 2022-Ohio-254 went back to the Trial Court to determine if enough evidence existed for a jury to find recklessness. The Trial Court considered the expert's opinion but ruled there was still insufficient evidence to establish recklessness and the claim was dismissed again and not appealed; Weglicki, supra Geauga C.P. NO 2021-6-0010.

This result means that if you ride in a bike club, or with a bike group, and you are injured by the actual or customary conduct of a fellow rider, even if negligent, you cannot recover against the offending cyclist unless that cyclist acted recklessly or intentionally.

This is why it's very important to have group rides that are regulated, supervised, and educated on safety. And again, it is crucial to announce intentions and inform the group when leaving a group ride. When a cyclist is leaving a group ride prematurely for whatever reason, they should tell the group and then drop to the back of the pack to make sure no other cyclist is riding behind who might be surprised at the stopping.

Case type: CYCLIST VS CYCLIST—TRIATHALON, PRIMARY ASSUMPTION OF THE RISK
***Wolf v. Kaplan*, 2021-Ohio-2447, 2021 Ohio App. LEXIS 2406**

During the Cleveland triathlon in 2018, Wolf and Kaplan were both participants. During the bicycle portion of this triathlon race, Kaplan allegedly violated the no drafting rule and caused Wolf to crash and sustain serious physical injuries. The Eighth District Court of Appeals affirmed the lower court ruling dismissing the case, holding that Kaplan's conduct was a foreseeable and customary risk of the sport of triathlon, and that the doctrine of primary assumption of the risk applied.

As a matter of law, the alleged conduct cannot be intentional or reckless. A participant in a recreational or sport activity assumes the ordinary risks and cannot recover for an injury without showing that the other participant's action was either reckless or intentional. The underlying rationale is to strike a balance between encouraging vigorous and free participation in recreational sports activities, while ensuring the safety of the players.

So, if you're injured by conduct that is a foreseeable, customary part of the sport, you have no case. The only case you can bring is when the actor is intentional; when they believe that the consequences are substantially certain to result in injury. The court held that recklessness in the context of a sporting event is different than ordinary recklessness. In other words, the acts must occur outside of normal conduct and customs of the sport. For instance, drinking alcohol is not part of the sport of bicycling, and liability will attach to an injury caused by alcohol use.

To me, the best analogy for these rulings is that they're like a football game where various penalties and rule infractions occur that are foreseeable parts of the game or competition. Liability will only attach when the violation is intentional rule violation and injury is foreseeable, such as a player taking off his helmet and using it to bash a helmetless player in the head.

Is flying down a hill well over the speed limit on a mixed group ride reckless? Likely. Is flying down the all purpose trail over the 15 mph speed limit left of center on a blind curve reckless? Maybe. Be careful out there—announce your intentions, warn other riders about what you are doing, stay observant, use hand signals! **Communicate!**

Case type: CYCLIST VS CYCLIST ORGANIZATION, EXPRESS ASSUMPTION OF THE RISK
Goss v. USA Cycling, Inc., 2022 - Ohio – 2500

Remember the NEOCycle held down at Edgewater Park? It involved numerous cycling events and races. Goss was a participant injured in a race and she sued the entities and person running the event who were responsible for setting up the racecourses. She alleged the racecourse was not in compliance with normal racecourses, that it was unsafe and poorly designed by amateurs.

Goss signed a waiver that recognized that cycling was an inherently dangerous sport waiving injury claims, even for negligence. The Trial Court dismissed the case, and the Eighth District Court of Appeals affirmed the dismissal because of her express assumption of risk via the waiver she signed.

Here we have another form of assumption of the risk: express assumption of the risk. When you sign a waiver, even for negligence, chances are it could bar claims against the race organizers.

07

FOR THE MOTORIST

WHY WE CYCLISTS DO WHAT WE DO!

*What the **** is that cyclist doing?!*

This section is for the motorist. As we all know, misunderstanding can sometimes create the wrong idea. For instance, bike maneuvers that appear illogical to a motorist may have a perfectly valid reason for occurring.

A word of caution about this section: What follows you may disagree with, and the actions you read about may not be entirely legal yet may be **entirely practical**. We pause from the legal theme for a moment to address some real-world bike behavior and lend a perspective that might help you understand **why** you're seeing it. A little more understanding might foster a little more patience. Why? Because everyone wants to get home safely no matter what vehicle they're operating. To that end, the following is some behavior you might see displayed by your two-wheeled cousins of the road, and why they do it.

Why are those cyclists riding in a pack like that? They're taking up the whole road!

It's easy to forget how nearly effortless it seems to cruise along at 25+ mph in your motor vehicle. In fact, it often feels down-right slow traveling at that speed, even though 25 mph is the upper limit on a significant number of our roads. Strong cyclists can cruise along at, or near this speed, but most can't.

Did you know that wind is the cause of roughly 80% of the resistance a cyclist feels while on their bike? This is where group riding comes in! That's right, drafting (aka sitting on a wheel, or slip streaming) isn't just for NASCAR—it's just as important in cycling. On average (depending on the speed) it takes roughly one-quarter less effort and energy to maintain a speed above 20 mph if another rider is blocking the wind by riding in front of you. The faster you go, the greater the effect.[87] This is the main reason you see those *Tour de France* types riding in a single line almost on top of each other; the leader who is "pulling" is taking the brunt of the wind, allowing the others to use less energy while matching his or her speed in their draft.

Because the lead rider is taking all the wind, they tend to tire more quickly and need to take a break. So, all the riders in the group typically take turns swapping off as leader, allowing the group as a whole to maintain a speed that may otherwise be unattainable for any individual rider.

Sometimes, particularly in places like the Cleveland Metroparks[88] you'll find groups of four, six, eight, or more cyclists drafting like this in a double file configuration. Some people assume that they're blocking the lane, but when you see this, you should understand that it's far easier and safer for a motorist to pass a compact group of riders rolling along two abreast than it is to pass the same number of riders in a single long line. If you're passing safely, the shorter the overall line of riders, the shorter the time you spend alongside them while facing oncoming traffic.

As a motorist, what should you do? Be patient, wait for a clear sight line, and pass the group of cyclists the same as you would pass any other slow-moving vehicle such as a bus or a buggy. A group such as this is aware of your presence, likely will have verbally alerted the rest of the group by shouting "car back" or "passing" and is wanting you to be out of that position on the road as much as you are!

Stop Signs and Group Riding

As for groups of cyclists going through stop signs together, riding through one by one would hold things up for motorists and drive everyone crazy. Again, not 100% legal, but it's a courtesy to all out in traffic when the cyclists stop and start as a whole group. In a well-known 2015 protest, cyclists in San Francisco responded to a police crackdown against their "rolling" stop signs by doing precisely what the law prescribes, i.e., individual riders each coming to a full and complete stop at the stop signs on a popular urban route called The Wiggle.

The results were predictably chaotic, with motorists blaring horns and yelling because of the delay caused by the increased congestion created when people on bikes followed a law that was promulgated for motor vehicles.[89] That said, best practice looks like everyone coming to a complete stop **as a group** with one foot down, then everyone proceeding **as a group**.

Finally, many motorists might encounter a cyclist or group of cyclists and without even thinking, overtake them, regardless of whether it's safe for oncoming traffic. This is common in the Cleveland Metroparks, which has multiple blind corners. A motorist should never pass a cyclist or a group of cyclists unless they can do so safely![90] Never pass a group of cyclists on a blind curve!

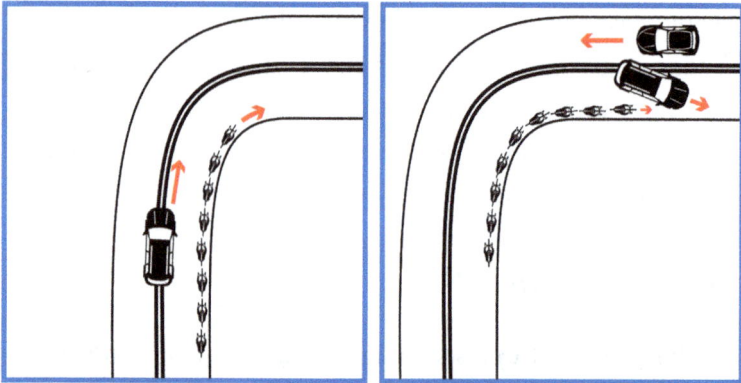

Examples of motorists unsafely passing cyclists on blind curves

Even when an oncoming motorist, lawfully in their lane with the right of way, is facing a motor vehicle on the wrong side of the road unsafely passing a group of cyclists (as in illustration B), this lawful motorist should **still try to get out of the way** by moving to the right and letting the oncoming vehicle safely pass all cyclists. The cyclists are not doing anything wrong, yet they are the ones most at risk if motor vehicles collide! Also, when passing a cyclist or group of cyclists, watch out for oncoming cyclists!

Why do cyclists point at the road?

There's one other very common signal you'll see cyclists perform when you encounter a group: pointing rather deliberately at the ground. What are they pointing at? Usually potholes, but it could be any surface. What feels like a mere jarring pothole in your motor vehicle would almost certainly cause a bike rider to crash if they were to hit it. How do cyclists deal with this reality when they're in a group? The lead riders point out surface hazards so the rest of the group can avoid them.

Hazard Hand Signal

A cyclist is standing on both pedals, but they seem stopped . . . what's up with that?

When a cyclist is standing balanced on their pedals while stopped at a red light, they're "track standing." This position of readiness for the experienced cyclist allows them to start moving again more quickly when the light changes. Admittedly, this can be confusing to motorists, especially those who aren't also cyclists. While it's an advanced skill for a cyclist to try, it's probably better if they make clear their intention of stopping by putting at least one foot on the ground.

"Filtering"

As mentioned in the last chapter, sometimes a cyclist will ride up the side of single lane traffic queued at a red light and position themselves at the front of the line. You have likely seen this as well. Absent a bike lane, this may not be technically correct (depending on the circumstances), and cyclists are generally supposed to wait in line like a motor vehicle[91 & 92] but practical reasons exist for filtering. Specifically, some cyclists think they are more visible positioned at the front of the line rather than being "buried" in a line of much larger vehicles which can obscure the cyclist's presence. Also, by being first and anticipating when the light changes, the cyclist is able to clear the intersection more quickly in a more visible manner. Given the high crash rates at those locations, this might be safer for the cyclist. Also, the cyclist may be stopped on an incline and moving up to the light on level ground can give them better ability to clip in and start more easily. Personally, I don't recommend filtering, unless there is a bike lane.

I don't see that stuff much . . . I see cyclists jumping lights and stop signs, and it makes me mad.

We could cite the statistics showing that people break the law on the roads at similar rates regardless of the vehicle they choose, but that isn't the point. By no means do we condone illegal conduct in any way. We're merely attempting to shed light on **why** such behavior exists. Even though bikes are co-equal vehicles under the law, some traffic engineers have historically ignored cyclists and share some of the blame for creating an environment where cyclists feel marginalized and not part of the system. And what do people do when they don't feel like they're a part of something? They tend to ignore some of its rules and defining characteristics. We need to build a more inclusive system with rules better designed for people on bikes. Other places in the United States are already doing so.

Idaho lawmakers first legalized the "Idaho Stop" in 1982—the first law in the United States allowing cyclists to treat stop signs as yields and red lights as stop signs—and cycling advocates as well as cities and states around the country have endorsed these ideas. A cyclist has a much better vantage point from a traffic control device like a red light or a stop sign than that of a motorist. In 2017 the state of Delaware approved a variation applying only to stop signs and referred to as the Delaware Yield. Colorado passed a law standardizing Idaho Stop/Stop-as-yield language for optional use by a county or municipality in 2018. In April 2019 Arkansas was the third state to add a version of the Idaho Stop to their laws,[93] followed by Oregon's Stop as Yield in June 2019.[94] Washington's Safety Stop was added in March 2020.[95] Oklahoma's Idaho Stop was signed into law in May 2021,[96] Utah's Utah Yield/Idaho Stop passed in March 2021 (after **five tries** since 2011!) and North Dakota added a Stop-as-Yield like Oregon's to their law in 2021.[97]

A handful of other states are working toward adopting a version of the Idaho Stop including California, which in August 2021 passed Bicycle Safety Stop legislation in its Senate.[98] In February 2022 the Illinois legislature vote against the Idaho Stop was nearly unanimous[99] which is a shame considering that just one year after its 1982 passage, Idaho saw a 14% drop in bicycle injuries and, fast-forwarding 28 years, ranked 30% better than "comparable peers" regarding bike safety. I hope Ohio adopts some version of the Idaho Stop as law.

The bottom line is that a cyclist has a better view of traffic when stopped at a light or stop sign, especially at a three-way intersection.

08

MOTORIST
RESPONSIBILITIES

DISTRACTED DRIVING, DOORING AND DEFENSIVE DRIVING

HUMANS ARE TERRITORIAL and instinctual by nature. Motorists focus on their destinations and tend to loathe obstructions and delays. A minority of them openly detest cyclists, to the point of suggesting that an injured or killed cyclist "got what they deserved" for riding on the road, even though a cyclist's right to do so is authorized and sanctioned by Ohio Law.

Distracted Driving

People who ride after dark or commute know how scary it is to see the "glowing faces" of people behind the wheels of their motor vehicles, illuminated by their cellphone screens as they are looking down at their phones rather than devoting their full attention to the act of driving. Bike crashes are often the result of motorists driving while distracted: texting, talking on cell phones, emailing, even watching movies while behind the wheel! Phone use in general creates dangerous issues for cyclists around motorists. This modern phone usage is much more dangerous than merely talking on the phone because the person texting is literally looking down or otherwise taking their eyes off the road. It is often referred to as the "new drunk driving".

Safety officials have taken increased actions over the past several years:

- A 2019 report by the National Transportation Safety Board (NTSB) called for eliminating distractions as a "most wanted" safety improvement and for banning all personal electronic device usage on our roadways throughout the nation[100] and on June 10, 2021, the NTSB appeared before the Ohio House of Representatives Committee on Criminal Justice regarding House Bill 283, which would prohibit use of personal electronic communications devices while driving. As you will soon read, these efforts paid off!

- According to the Ohio Department of Transportation (ODOT), between 2013 and 2017 there were nearly 66,000 crashes in Ohio due to distracted driving;[101] the Ohio State Highway Patrol reported another 65,298 distracted driving crashes from the beginning of January 2018 to mid-July 2023[102]

- Research has shown that spending a mere five seconds texting—the amount of time the average text takes to send—at 55 mph, is the equivalent of driving a football field's entire length **with your eyes closed!**[103]

FINALLY, UPDATED DISTRACTED DRIVING LAWS!

Distracted Driving—Secondary Offense

As mentioned in Chapter Three, Ohio's "secondary offense" distracted driving legislation, Ohio Revised Code §4511.991, became effective in October 2018 and was updated on April 4, 2023. Broadly defined, "distracted driving" is: *Engaging in any activity that is not necessary to the operation of a vehicle and impairs, or reasonably would be expected to impair, the ability of the operator to drive the vehicle safely.* If law enforcement believes that a motorist is distracted while committing a moving violation, and that the distraction is a contributing factor to the moving violation, the motorist is subject to an additional fine.[104]

This law made distracted driving a secondary offense, not a primary offense, meaning that a police officer could not pull a motorist over for distracted driving independently of another primary violation (such as speeding or failing to obey a traffic control device). A first violation will result in a misdemeanor.

Primary Offense!

Ohio's "Driving while Texting" law, Ohio Revised Code §4511.204[105] became effective April 4, 2023. This statute makes holding cell phones and other electronic communications devices while driving a **primary** traffic offense for all drivers. Law enforcement can now pull over and cite a texting driver **without** the driver committing another primary traffic offense, such as running a red light. There are over 10 exceptions, however, including hands-free use and emergency calls.

Solid proof that combined efforts of constituents and lawmakers can yield powerful results! This new legislation is an important step in improving safety for all road users, regardless of how they use them.

"Dooring"

An issue for cyclists and motorists, "dooring" occurs when a motorist in a parked vehicle opens their driver's side door without first checking to see if anyone (such as a cyclist) is passing on the left. One way to ensure safe door opening is to employ a strategy originating in the Netherlands known as the "Dutch Reach." When preparing to exit a parked motor vehicle, reaching across the body to open the driver's side door with the **right** (far) hand rather than the left causes the body to pivot, providing an automatic view of the blind spot and who/what might be coming along the road from behind.

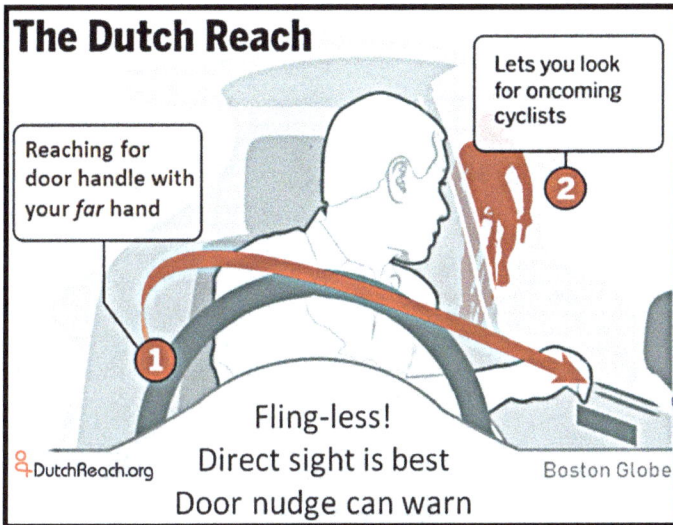

The Dutch Reach

Lets you look for oncoming cyclists

Reaching for door handle with your *far* hand

①

②

Fling-less!
Direct sight is best
Door nudge can warn

DutchReach.org

Boston Globe

Source: Dutch Reach Project

The Ohio Revised Code states that no person shall open the door on the side available to moving traffic **unless**, and **until** it is **reasonably safe** and can be done **without interfering** with the **movement** of other **traffic**. Violation of this statute results in a minor misdemeanor and a fine of up to $150[106] and on top of that, you may be liable to an injured party for medical expenses and bike repair or replacement. Attention, cyclists: If you are in a dooring crash caused by an unsafe motorist, be sure to get that motorist's driver license, license plate and insurance info, just as you would if involved in any other bike crash! While the adrenaline is pumping, you might not realize the extent of your injuries.

The point here is that it is incumbent upon motorists to ensure that it's 100% safe when opening their driver's side doors. So, why not give the Dutch Reach a try? Then, share it with everyone you know who drives a motor vehicle!

What is "Defensive Driving"? How can it help avoid crashes with cyclists and pedestrians?

Idioms get thrown around a lot in our society and the same applies to the phrase "defensive driving". Sports analogies can be useful. You've probably heard the phrase "the best defense is a good offense". We all know what defense and offense mean in the NFL, but how do those terms translate when we're behind the wheel? Read on to discover how the opposite of this popular idiom—i.e., "the best offense is a good defense"—can work in our favor as motorists.

To understand what it means to drive "defensively" let's first explore what it means to drive "offensively." In the NFL, it's the offense who has control. They make all the moves, they try to move forward, and they will run over or through anyone who gets in their path. Sound familiar? We've all seen them on the road, offensive drivers who do not care about other motorists, pedestrians, or cyclists. They have one goal and one goal only, getting to their destination as quickly as possible. And sometimes, with little to no regard for safety.

So, what is defensive driving? Simply put, it's the opposite of offensive driving. Instead of charting a path and charging forward with no regard for what others are doing, the defensive driver continually identifies what is going on around their vehicle and continually adjusts so that **visibility** and **space** are maximized, thus giving themselves **time to react and adjust** in a dangerous situation so that **crashes are avoided**, period.

Here's the good news . . . if you are currently an offensive driver (this may take some honest self-assessment), the transition to becoming a defensive driver is simply a matter of choice. While the new skills and habits may take some time to develop, they are relatively simple. Let's look at a few key techniques for becoming a defensive driver and exploring how they can be used to protect yourself, other motorists, cyclists, and pedestrians. The good news is that it could save the life of a cyclist or pedestrian **and** keep you out of court.

Heavyweight Fight? No Contest!

How much do you weigh? Okay, impolite question. Let's assume you're of average human weight (or thereabouts) and you weigh between 125 and 250 pounds (depending upon many factors, of course).

Now, how much does a bicycle weigh? Again, depending upon numerous factors, a bike's weight can range anywhere from 17 to 80 pounds–approximately the same range as the luggage you carry to the airport.

Okay, how about your car, truck, or SUV? Now we're talking about weight that is literally in tons. One ton is equal to 2,000 pounds. A small car or crossover will start out at 2,000 pounds, minimum, and that's before you load it with fuel, cargo, and people. Larger cars and medium-sized SUVs will easily hit 4,000 pounds on the scale–empty–and full-sized pickup trucks can roll off the assembly line at 5,000 pounds or more. That's two-and-a-half tons! Fully loaded, a Ford F150 will top the scales at around 6,500 pounds, or three-and-a-quarter tons! And we haven't even hooked up a utility, camper, or boat/trailer yet–add up to another 8,000 pounds (four tons) or more to that total package, depending upon the vehicle and equipment.

What's the point here? The point is that when you're behind the wheel of a modern car, crossover, light truck, or SUV, **there is no contest** when it comes to weight class. A 200-pound human walking down the street or riding a bicycle which weighs between 17 and 80 pounds stands **no chance whatsoever** against even the smallest vehicles on the road today. If it were a prize fight, it would be over with one swing from the heavyweight. And the kinetic energy produced as a function of speed can easily kill.

As a defensive driver, it's critical that these key elements of mass, kinetic energy, and physics are not overlooked.

The Dangers of Distraction and Speed

How long does it take to read or send a text message–maybe five or six seconds? Surely that's not so bad when you consider how attentive you are when driving, right? What could go wrong?

It's useful to first understand just how far you travel in six seconds. At 25 mph, your vehicle will travel 36.6 feet per second (FPS), or a total distance of almost 220 feet. That's two-thirds the length of a football field. A **lot** can go wrong in that distance.

It gets worse at highway speed when your vehicle is easily traveling at 70 mph. You're traversing the length of a football field in **less** than three seconds. Every three seconds, an entire football field! So, if you look down at your phone for six seconds, you've just gone the distance of two football fields, end zone to end zone, or over $1/10^{th}$ of a mile.

Still feel good about sending that text? It can wait. And it's not just cell phones, **any** distraction that takes your **eyes** off the road, your **hands** off the wheel, or your **mind** off the task of driving is classified as a distraction under Ohio Law.

Driving Defensively to Identify Cyclists and Pedestrians

Let's assume you're sold on the concept of managing distractions while driving. Great! You're on your way to becoming a defensive driver. Now, let's take it to the next level . . .

The best way to avoid striking a pedestrian or cyclist is to identify them **well before** your vehicle gets close enough to hit them. You can do this by employing three key defensive driving practices:

- Looking ahead: A common practice covered in nearly every quality defensive driving instruction curriculum. Basically, the concept is to "look up" higher than you normally do, while driving to the point down the road where your vehicle will be, eight to twelve seconds in the future. That's where your **eyes** should be focusing, conditions permitting. If you do this consistently you will identify most hazards, including cyclists and pedestrians, with plenty of time to react to their presence to avoid a crash.

- Keeping head and eyes moving: This turns your sense of sight essentially into a "radar" continuously moving left and right as you proceed down the road, "scanning" for anything that could pose the risk of a crash and giving you plenty of time to react. Identifying cyclists or pedestrians you may have missed using the "Looking Ahead" concept will give you ample opportunity to react to their presence. Though less critical for freeway driving, it is very important in urban environments, parking lots, or anywhere pedestrians and/or cyclists may be present.

- No tailgating–maintain safe following distance: Ohio is in the top 10 in the U.S. for tailgating violations!

This can be one of the toughest habits to change for the driver who has already adopted a defensive posture. In defensive driving classes of the past, a recommendation to measure safe following distance was by car lengths–usually one car length per 10 miles per hour of speed. However, if we assume the average car or light truck is 20 feet long (they are usually shorter than that), at 70 miles per hour the recommended safe following distance would be 140 feet (7 x 20). At 70 mph, that's less than 1.5 seconds of following time, which is not **nearly** enough time to react if an emergency stop is required–not even by half. The only safe way to gauge proper following time/distance is to use the **timed interval rule**, which recommends three seconds of following time (not distance or car lengths) under normal driving conditions–more if the weather is inclement or traction is compromised.

In a nutshell, when the rear bumper of the vehicle you are following crosses any fixed point, at least three seconds should elapse before your front bumper reaches the same point. Simple, but takes some practice to gauge correctly. You'll note that the time is constant (three seconds) but the distance will change based upon speed, which takes some getting used to for most drivers. But, if followed, **this one defensive driving concept** can help increase the view ahead, identify pedestrians and cyclists early, and prevent many serious crashes.

Preventability and Right of Way

You're driving down the road, minding your own business and employing the concepts of defensive driving by managing distractions, looking 8-12 seconds down the road to identify hazards, and scanning continuously in case you missed something. But suddenly, **there they are**! A pedestrian or cyclist in your path who seemingly came out of nowhere, as the saying goes. Now what?!

You have the right of way, let's assume. You may have a clear path, a green light, no light at all, or any other legal indicator of proceeding unabated. But now this pedestrian or cyclist is there, in your way, obstructing your path, clearly in danger. What should you do?

Let's go back to that discussion about weight. Your vehicle weighs at least a ton, possibly three tons or more. Striking that pedestrian or cyclist could easily result in their death and certainly serious injury. Would it be your **fault**? Would you be liable for their death, or cleared because you had the right of way?

Well, Ohio has comparative fault and if a jury finds you are 50% or more at fault, you are on the hook! Even if you may or may not be legally liable, **preventability** comes into play. Could you have prevented the crash by doing everything in your power to stop it from happening, regardless of who had the right of way? You could be 50% or more at fault even if you had the right of way. More importantly, do you have the right to execute someone who intentionally or unintentionally obstructed your path of travel? Reasonable people would say "absolutely not" because the punishment doesn't fit the crime. We all make mistakes, and the greater responsibility–as a human–should rest with the one who has the most power.

In this case, it's the person behind the wheel. Don't take chances with human lives. Neither your own, nor those of others!

09

BIKE *(& PEDESTRIAN)* CRASHES

AWARENESS, CONSEQUENCES AND PREVENTION

WHEN YOU LOOK AT THE NUMBER of people cycling versus the number of injuries, cycling is generally safe in Ohio. However, bike crashes do occur, and protected bike lanes aren't always available. Those who practice "vehicular cycling"—i.e., riding their bike like they drive their motor vehicle—are in 75-80% fewer crashes! Awareness on the part of both motorists and cyclists can go a long way in helping to prevent bike/auto crashes. Riding your bike in this manner usually gives a cyclist the right of way (ROW), or the right to proceed uninterruptedly. As a cyclist, you want to "ROW"!

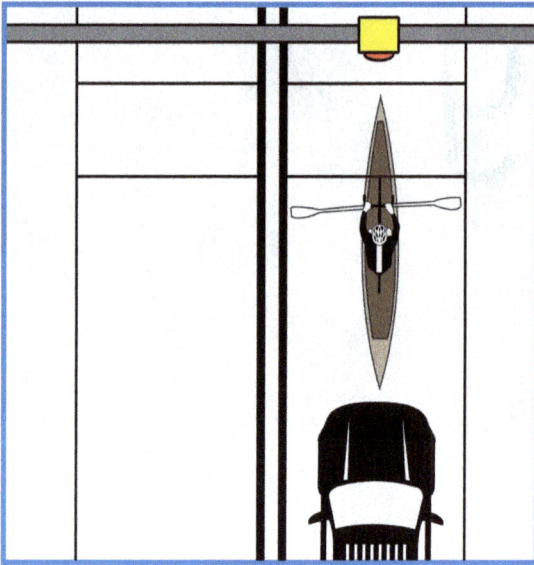

Right of Way (ROW)

Causes and Types of Bike Crashes

The bike crash types we generally encounter have names:

- The **Rear Ender**: Just how it sounds, a motor vehicle crashes into a cyclist from behind.

- The **Left Cross**: A left angle crash during which a motor vehicle turns left, directly in front of an oncoming cyclist.

- The **Right Hook**, Part One: A right angle crash during which a motor vehicle passes a cyclist, then turns right directly in front of the cyclist.

- **The Right Hook**, Part Two: A right angle crash during which a cyclist on the right is passing a slower-moving or stopped motor vehicle on the cyclist's left, and the motor vehicle suddenly turns right, directly into the cyclist.

You'll notice that most of these are turning maneuvers which occur at intersections, locations that require extra care and attention.

What should motorists do to avoid a bike crash?

It's simple. Motorists **should** remain aware and be on the lookout for people on bikes, not just for people in motor vehicles, and **shouldn't** drive distractedly! Motorists should also realize that **bicycles are legal road vehicles with the right of way**, so when you're pulling out of your driveway, wait for a bike to safely pass, as you would for any other vehicle with the right of way. (See Defensive Driving in Chapter Eight.)

What can a cyclist do?

Cyclists should also remain aware and focused. Follow the rules of the road. Be predictable and announce your intentions. Be on the lookout for other road users.

Beyond that—and particularly around intersections—if cycling on a narrow street, cyclists should consider taking the full (whole) lane by moving toward the center of the lane; this could help to prevent anyone in a motor vehicle from passing too closely to the cyclist on the left or potentially right-hook-ing them. Moreover, an oncoming, left-turning motorist may have a clearer view of the approaching cyclist because the cyclist is positioned where motorists typically look for other motor vehicles.

Ken Taking the Full Lane

All Purpose Trails in the Metroparks and CVNP

Multi-use paths are marked shared paths for runners, walk-ers, families, and us cyclists!

If you're riding on the all purpose trail in the Metroparks or Cuyahoga Valley National Park (CVNP), try to get off the trail when stopping or if having an issue with your bike. Be careful to look for oncoming cyclists if riding two abreast, and if you **are** riding two abreast—move out of the way of an oncoming cyclist. Obey the center line of the trail if one is present, and if not, treat the trail as if it has an imaginary center line and don't cross over unless it's safe. Be especially careful not to cross over on a blind curve with potential oncoming cyclists. Try to announce your intentions when passing, e.g., "Passing on the left" or "Riders passing on the left" if you're first to pass in a group. You can also use a bell to warn when passing. In a nutshell: Be courteous—warn when passing—stay to the right except when passing but even then, try not to go left of the center line.

The "Stobbe Shout": Pretend You're Invisible! Don't Assume a Motorist Sees You

Gary Stobbe and I grew up on Cleveland's west side. He attended Holy Name, I went to Ignatius, and we played football against each other for four years (split two and two). What that has to do with this book is perplexing, but I thought it was fun to share!

Gary drove a '68 Chevy with no working horn. (Back in the day, motor vehicles were often mechanically challenged!) In situations that called for honking, often Gary would simply shout—loudly—and motorists would actually hear him and stop. The "Stobbe Shout" was born.

Gary Stobbe today!

This can be as useful today as it was in the '70s. Pretend you are invisible! Never assume a motorist sees you! Consider using the Stobbe Shout to help "wake up" a motorist from their inattention. Things happen quickly on the road, and depending on the situation, the Stobbe Shout (or other verbal or hand alert of some kind) could be useful. However, this is obviously not a legal requirement by any means, but an additional tactic a cyclist may employ to stay safer.

Pedestrians and Unsafe Drivers

Vehicle size also contributes to pedestrian risk. Approximately 75% of new vehicles in the truck/SUV/van categories boast increasing size and speed, making them an even greater hazard to other road users. The Governors Highway

Safety Association reported that since 2011 the pedestrian crash fatality rate has grown 46%, a huge disparity over the 5% increase for all other crashes.[107] A report from the Ohio State Highway Patrol dated October 2022 shows that pedestrian-related crashes in the state totaled a whopping 14,466 between 2017 and 2022.[108] Regarding the City of Cleveland, as of this writing the most recent information from Vision Zero Cleveland with info obtained from the Ohio Department of Transportation (ODOT) Geographic Crash Analysis Tool (GCAT) is 252 pedestrian crashes in the city between 2016-2020.[109]

Whatever vehicle we drive, it's an issue that affects us all.

10

CYCLIST HIT BY AN UNSAFE MOTORIST

IMPORTANT STEPS

THERE USUALLY isn't any warning before a crash, so adopt the Boy Scouts of America's motto and "Be Prepared!"

Beyond maintaining awareness, an important part of our duty as cyclists is to have **a plan for coping with a crash**, should one unfortunately occur. To that end I've created a handy acronym— "PHONE":

P is for **Police**: Call the police and **insist** on a report, **no matter what**; you need documentation! **Always** call the police, even if the motorist begs you not to and/or seems like a saint or even if the police try to talk you out of filing a report.

If you don't, the lack of a record and documentation of the crash will cause you suffering later! Some police like to give careless motorists a break. **If possible, don't let them!** Always request that the officer cites the motorist for the appropriate traffic offense.

H is for **Healthcare**: Seek immediate medical attention for **all** injuries.

O is for **Observe/Obtain**: Get the motorist's contact and insurance info, and names of all witnesses, or try to make sure the police or other witnesses or bystanders obtain this vital information.

N is for **Notification**: Call an experienced bike injury attorney (me!) **before** you talk to the at fault motorist's liability adjuster. The adjusters are pros for the insurance companies—hire a pro for yourself! Remember, the liability adjuster for the motorist is **not** on your side and will likely be calling you within 48 hours of the crash.

The at fault insurance company's representative may pressure you for information and possibly into **agreeing to terms that may not even come close to covering all damages.** Never sign or agree to sign a settlement before consulting with an attorney, because you may be inadvertently waiving your right to pursue legal action to recover the full amount for your injuries and you may have to live with your rash decision for the rest of your life. For an example, see *Bailey v. Vaughn*, 2017-Ohio-7725 (Ct. App.)[110] in Chapter Thirteen.

E is for **Evidence**: After a crash, try to be your own legal reporter and document in detail all you can see and recall until police arrive on the scene. Don't let the at fault party move their motor vehicle **or** your bicycle before the police arrive.

Look for a building security camera that may have recorded the crash.

Be sure to keep all damaged property (without cleaning or repairing it) including, for example, the bike frame, ripped clothing and accessories, and make sure you check the inside and outside of your cracked helmet for signs of head impact that may not be remembered or apparent to you in the moments after a crash.

Take pictures with your cell phone of the motor vehicle, your damaged bike, ripped clothing, and cuts and abrasions! These items are **valuable pieces of evidence**. In the moments after being hit this can be particularly difficult, but if you're able, this is an important step. If you have a modern GPS-enabled bicycle computer such as a Garmin or a Wahoo, check the data for the actual speed and location of where the crash took place, and let your attorney know if you have ride footage from a GoPro-type camera.[111] These cameras, along with non-mandated daytime lights, are a growing trend among cyclists as they take additional steps in an attempt to protect themselves. Tell your attorney if you are on Strava or MapMyRide or a similar ride app so your information can be downloaded. And as soon as you can, start keeping a daily journal of symptoms, treatments, days off work, etc. This documentation will give your attorney a detailed picture of the impact the careless driver is having on your life. Once you've started a treatment plan such as physical therapy, it's best to attend all sessions and avoid "gaps" in your treatment.

Knabe Law Firm[112] has a supply of laminated PHONE business cards you can easily carry in your jersey pocket to help you remember the important steps to take in the event of a crash. Please contact our office to request a complementary card be mailed to you. The reverse side of these cards lists a "**Cyclist's Arsenal**" with current Ohio bike laws that all cyclists should have at their fingertips while out on the road.

Time is of the essence after a crash. Time gaps between the crash and your seeking medical or legal services can have an impact on your case. Again, as soon as possible, contact an experienced personal injury attorney who specializes in bike crashes. Legal services are like medical services in this regard. If you have a specific medical condition, you don't only see a general practitioner—you make an appointment with a specialist. When it comes to bikes and the law, that's me. I've attended countless depositions and have had numerous bike injury cases in which the defense attorney lacked even the most basic knowledge of cycling and the various (and sometimes expensive) components that make up a bike; nor did they understand a rider's array of personal equipment, or how cyclists ride in single/double pace lines, how they draft, how GPS-type equipment may shed additional light on a case, and so much more. My specializations combining extensive riding experience, bike safety advocacy, and legal expertise offer a huge advantage for my clients.

11

. . . .

DAMAGES IN A BIKE/AUTO CRASH

MORE THAN YOU MIGHT THINK!

PHYSICAL INJURIES are often the first thing we think of, after a bike crash. A cyclist on a 15- to 50-pound bike **never** wins in a crash with a 2,000-pound box! Injuries are usually serious and no laughing matter, but as the old joke goes, "What about the bike?!

Bike, Component and Accessory Damages

Property damage is almost guaranteed in any bike crash where fault is not an issue. Bikes aren't mere toys and can cost thousands of dollars! A damaged bike frame, components, and accessories are often costly, and damage to these items can also be critically important evidence. Not to mention the expensive smartphone you're likely carrying. **Documentation is key!** A reputable bike shop will help in establishing fair dollar value for bike, component, and accessory damages. Most liability insurance carriers will pay a bike property damage claim if the estimates are accurate and backed up by a written estimate from a bike shop along with clear damage photos.

To make an uninsured motorist claim in Ohio (that is, a claim against your own auto policy because the other party was uninsured) you need independent corroborative evidence of a hit-and-run crash. In addition to an eyewitness, the bike frame, component, or accessory damage may constitute that evidence. Check the frame for paint transfer stains from the hit-and-run motorist's vehicle.

Economic & Non-Economic Damages: Medical/Lost Wages and Pain/Suffering/ Disability

In addition to compensation for bike and accessory damage, injured cyclists are entitled to **separate sums** for both **economic** and **non-economic** damages. Allow me to explain.

Economic losses/damages generally consist of medical bills and loss of income. This is normally easy to calculate using simple math.

Non-economic losses are more nebulous to calculate because they include things like "pain and suffering". **Pain** is the neurological response to physical injury to the body, and **suffering** is psychological, meaning a mental or emotional state brought on by the injury such as nervousness, grief, anxiety, worry, shock, humiliation, and indignity. **Basic losses** include the inability to perform the daily activities of life such as walking, lifting, climbing stairs, feeding oneself, or driving a motor vehicle. **Pleasurable losses** include the inability to engage in activities that a person enjoyed prior to the injury such as hobbies, recreational activities, and sports.

Non-economic damages are capped in Ohio, but exceptions exist including when a cyclist suffers a permanent substantial deformity injury.

Substantial injuries including broken bones and other serious, long-lasting physical injuries commonly occur when cyclists are hit by motor vehicles. Concussions are common even among those wearing helmets. Post-Concussion Syndrome can include dizziness, confusion, light sensitivity, noise sensitivity, headaches, memory loss and/or hearing loss. Traumatic Brain Injuries (TBIs) occur all too frequently during bike crashes and can have an irreparable impact on a person's life. It's important to understand that while people often mistake a concussion for a minor injury, they are much more serious. In his article "An Overview of Traumatic Brain Injury," EMT-Paramedic Rod Brouhard states, "You can have TBI with or without a concussion, but you can't have a concussion without TBI."[113]

Cleveland Cyclist Ashley Shaw's Story

Ashley Shaw is a Cleveland resident living in Ohio City, a historic neighborhood on the near west side. In 2017, she was motor vehicle-free by choice and riding her bike a mere block from home when she was hit by a motor vehicle, causing her to sustain a TBI in the form of a subdural hematoma, aka a "brain bleed". She remembers only silence for the first several days after the crash, a silence that "will always stay with (her)".

For the first year, Shaw's post-crash symptoms included noticeably slower speech and difficulty forming sentences, both verbally and in writing. She continues to experience short term memory loss, fatigue, nausea, light sensitivity, and issues with balance and falling. Perhaps most difficult of all is that despite appearing "healthy" to those around her, unseen symptoms of Post-Traumatic Stress Disorder (PTSD)[114] are part of her experience, more often than not. Stressful situations—even simple everyday actions such as crossing a street—can be overwhelming, triggering her brain and sympathetic nervous system to activate the "fight-or-flight mode". In her own words, several times a day her body feels "as if it's being chased by a bear."

All this, due to a motorist not paying attention behind the wheel.

Despite these ongoing challenges, Shaw has been able to move forward, first as Chief Operating Officer and Director of Neighborhood Planning at Ohio City Incorporated,[115] and as of this writing as Executive Director of MidTown Cleveland, Inc.[116] She also co-chaired the City of Cleveland's past Vision Zero Enforcement Subcommittee. She's grateful for the opportunity this difficult life experience has offered her. In her own words:

"Something really unexpected happens when you have a close call with your life. It puts the important things into perspective . . . I value my life, my experiences, and my relationships in a completely different way than I did before. My life now is simple and slow, but so much more meaningful. I am one of the lucky ones."[117]

12

············

INSURANCE FOR CYCLISTS

HOW CAN INSURANCE PROTECT CYCLISTS?

DISCLAIMER: The information shared in this chapter is general. Each situation is uniquely fact based and each insurance policy is an individual contract, with specific language and exclusions varying from company to company.

What happens when an at fault cyclist hits a pedestrian or motor vehicle?

- The cyclist is **not** covered under the cyclist's auto liability policy; **but**

- The cyclist should be covered under the cyclist's homeowner or renter policy per the liability section (if there are no written exclusions).

What happens when a cyclist is hit by an at fault motorist who has no liability insurance coverage?

Just because Ohio law requires insurance to drive, don't assume a driver who hits a cyclist has insurance coverage, because many don't. Anyone can simply check the box that says they have liability insurance! No proof is required until the driver is pulled over.

The cyclist should be covered by the **uninsured motorist** protection under **the cyclist's own personal auto policy**, assuming the cyclist purchased this coverage known as **"U coverage"**.

What happens when a cyclist is hit by an at fault motorist who has inadequate insurance?

The cyclist should be covered under the cyclist's own **underinsured (UIM) motorist** protection in **their personal auto policy**; assuming the cyclist also has a motor vehicle for which they have purchased this coverage known as **"UIM coverage"** (as most cyclists also own motor vehicles). **For UIM to apply, the amount of the UIM coverage must exceed the liability limits of the at fault motorist's insurance policy.**

U coverage and UIM coverage are typically combined in an auto policy under U coverage, so make sure to check your policy to confirm both U and UIM are counted in your policy under U coverage. **Remember, a cyclist doesn't have "full coverage" unless the cyclist has U coverage!**

These days when folks are buying their auto insurance, they're often purchasing it online without professional advice. This is risky because all insurance coverage is simply not the same, and Ohio has eliminated the mandatory requirement of insurance companies offering U coverage.

The bottom line? Here is the coverage you should carry:

- All cyclists whose budget can allow for it **should** purchase U coverage under their personal auto liability policy to protect them if they are hit by an at fault motorist with the bare minimum, or no liability insurance; this coverage should also protect them if they are struck by a hit-and-run motorist, assuming there is independent corroborating evidence.

- All cyclists should consider purchasing a homeowner or renter insurance policy that covers the cyclist's potential liability in injuring a person or damaging property; it also could cover bike theft and/or bike damage if you are hit by an at fault uninsured motorist.

Can I purchase bike insurance separately from my auto insurance?

Cyclists with no homeowner, no renter, and/or no personal auto coverage may consider purchasing a separate bicycle insurance policy. You can obtain a quote and purchase a bicycle insurance policy online at Velosurance.[118]

Should I carry an umbrella under my policy?

"Umbrella" insurance is a type of insurance that covers liability claims in excess of your underlying auto or homeowner insurance limits. If you are at fault and injure someone, your liability umbrella coverage is important to prevent the injured party's collecting from your personal assets. Just as importantly, if it's offered, you should always elect U coverage under your umbrella policy in case you are injured by an underinsured or uninsured motorist whose coverage is inadequate to compensate you.

What if a cyclist has minimum U coverage?

Minimum coverage means minimum protection! You could run into trouble on your U coverage protection if you only have minimum coverage. Why? If your current U coverage is only $25,000 and the at fault motorist's liability coverage is $25,000, you can't collect more than $25,000 in insurance coverage no matter how badly you're hurt because your own coverage matches that of the at fault motorist, so you only collect from theirs. It is better than nothing, but medical bills can quickly exceed this minimum amount.

Remember: You cannot depend on the at fault motorist to carry enough liability coverage to protect you. Be prepared and protect yourself, if your budget allows, by buying **full and adequate coverage**—not minimum coverage! We recommend at least $100,000/$300,000 in liability and U coverages, or more if your budget permits. We also recommend purchasing umbrella coverage which **could** provide extra liability and U coverage.

Some insurance companies are advertising minimum coverage "for the rest of us." This tells us that many motorists likely only have minimum legal coverage and offers further reason for cyclists to purchase higher amounts of UIM coverage.

What about bike theft?

No cyclist wants to think about their bike getting stolen! However, if it happens, it's good to know that with most insurance companies your bike is covered under "personal property/contents" on your homeowner or renter policy, as long as it was taken from a known location. This coverage is subject to a deductible. If you've taken the extra step of "scheduling" your bike (scheduling means itemizing specific items of value to provide higher levels of protection), not only is it covered, but you also won't have to pay a deductible.

What about e-scooter coverage . . . or lack thereof?

E-scooters such as the ones in downtown Cleveland provided by companies like Bird and Lime are still somewhat new. These companies know how to protect themselves—they require users to sign an agreement assuming full responsibility for anything happening during the time of use. In other words, if an e-scooter rider crashes into someone, they are personally responsible for that person's injuries. If a rider crashes into a tree, causing damage to the e-scooter, they are personally responsible for that damage. **The rider always bears full responsibility for liability for anything occurring during their ride.**

The bottom line on scooter coverage: If you choose to ride e-scooters, don't depend on the e-scooter companies to provide you with insurance coverage! Protect yourself in all possible ways. Make sure you have homeowner or renter insurance, which may cover you if you hit someone or something. Make sure you have U coverage under your auto policy, to cover you if you are hit by a motorist. And check with your insurance agent about your coverage on e-scooters and other micro-mobility devices you may find yourself using.

13

OHIO BIKE
CASES

REAL STUFF!

THE FOLLOWING are Ohio bike cases, with real cyclists and real results. Read with care—you never know what may happen out on the road, but you **should** know what **could** happen!

Case type: CRIMINAL/TRAFFIC OFFENSE—CYCLIST
State v. Patrick (Ohio Municipal Court, 2008)[119]

Two cyclists were allegedly riding two abreast when a police officer in a marked cruiser confronted them. The officer felt they were impeding traffic and attempted to stop them verbally and with lights and siren. The cyclists did not comply and the officer "tased" one of them. The tased cyclist faced criminal misdemeanor charges in Lawrence County Municipal Court—Resisting Arrest, Disorderly Conduct, Operating a Bicycle in the Roadway, and Failure to Comply with a Police Order.

The Lawrence County Municipal Court judge found the cyclist "not guilty" since he'd committed no violations and no probable cause of a crime existed for the officer's stopping him and his fellow cyclist. A local authority (defined as every county, municipal, and other local board or body having authority to adopt police regulations under the constitution and laws of this state) cannot prohibit cyclists from riding on the road unless it's a closed or limited access highway or freeway. Since the police orders were not lawful, no duty existed requiring the cyclist to halt, and he had a fundamental right under the Fourth Amendment to be left alone.

This is an interesting case and I'm glad the cyclist won. However, not all judges or juries are as knowledgeable or as sympathetic as this judge. Cyclists can ride two abreast in Ohio. In fact, it is a common courtesy to do so, especially in the case of group riding since it can shorten the line of a larger group of riders. There is no requirement in the Ohio statute requiring cyclists to go single file to let traffic pass. Cyclists can also ride on most roads. That said, should a police officer order you to stop, it's often a good idea to comply. Getting tased is not worth it. Just make sure you know the law and your rights.

As I mentioned earlier, to help with this, available at my office are laminated PHONE bike cards containing all the laws that favor cyclists, including the right to ride on the road and two abreast! These free cards should be kept in your jersey pocket on every ride and presented to any police officer who may be unaware of the evolving laws regarding bicycles and cyclist rights.

Case type: CRIMINAL OFFENSE—CYCLIST
State v. Gatto (Ohio Court of Appeals, 2007)[120]

A fire chief driving an ambulance came upon a group of cyclists and ordered them to ride single file. One of the cyclists responded "Go **** yourself." The chief threatened to take further action, to which the cyclist allegedly responded that he should "Shove his radio up his ******* ***." The chief then alerted a police officer who cited the cyclist for disorderly conduct, and she was convicted at trial.

However, the 6th District Court of Appeals overturned the cyclist's conviction because even though she swore at the fire chief and upset him, her words did not amount to "fighting words" and were protected by the First Amendment (Amendment I). Cyclists can also ride two abreast in Ohio.

Obviously, I support this correct result. But this is an example of where the cyclist may have opted to either ignore the unlawful command from the fire chief, or simply respond more calmly. A cyclist's reaction oftentimes determines the outcome of an encounter with authorities and other road users. In this case, the cyclist was rightfully able to get her conviction overturned on appeal, but she had to go through hell to get it.

First edition reader and fellow attorney Ken Robinson provided the following feedback:

> "*I especially appreciated your explaining State v. Gatto, noting that, while the cyclist prevailed, she had to "go through hell" to get there. I believe many laypersons don't understand that avoiding the court proceeding in the first place is usually much more agreeable than winning it.*"

Case type: TRAFFIC OFFENSES—CYCLIST
State v. Tudor (Ohio Court of Appeals, 2019)[121]

At around 5:00 p.m. in August, a cyclist was riding his bike eastbound on Main Street in Ravenna's downtown commercial district. According to the police, this cyclist was riding "… in the center of the lane, holding a McDonald's cup in his left hand, and flapping or waving his right hand". The cyclist was charged with Reckless Operation of his bicycle, Obstructing Official Business and not Driving in Marked Lanes, all misdemeanor charges. The prosecutor did not pursue the Obstructing Official Business charge, but the municipal judge found the cyclist guilty of Reckless Operation. The cyclist appealed his conviction, but in a 2-1 decision, the 11th District Appellate Court of Portage County affirmed the lower court and upheld his conviction of Reckless Operation.

The Court reasoned that riding his bicycle with no hands while holding a cup on a commercial street compromised this cyclist's ability to steer the bicycle and to brake, and allegedly constituted a willful and wanton disregard for the safety of others. The cyclist argued that he was still able to maintain control of his bicycle and that no injury had occurred, but this argument failed to convince the majority of the Appellate judges.

The dissenting Appellate judge said the evidence showed that the cyclist had control of his bicycle, and since there were parked motor vehicles off to his right, the cyclist had every reason to ride closer to the center of the lane. Even though this cyclist may have been an inconvenience to motorists behind him, he posed no threat to the safety of any person or property.

The dissent correctly pointed out that there were motor vehicles parked to the cyclist's right and riding closer to the center of the lane was practicable to avoid being "doored" by someone exiting a motor vehicle. However, this was not the majority opinion and illustrates the uncertainty that can occur when bike cases go before a court. I've seen many cyclists who were in complete control while riding with no hands (although I'm not one of them, **kudos** to anyone who is) and drinking from a water bottle or fishing around for an energy bar in their back pocket. In this case, the aggravating circumstances of having a cup in one hand and waving the other while riding in a commercial district pushed the Court over the edge to convict this cyclist, but it could have gone the other way.

However, if the actions of this cyclist here were legally sufficient to establish Reckless Operation, a motorist driving while distracted is as much or more of a safety threat; the police and courts should consider distracted driving to be Reckless Operation under any interpretation of this case.

Case type: CRIMINAL OFFENSE—MOTORIST
State v. Copley (Ohio Court of Appeals, 2010)[122]

A motorist driving a van with three other occupants came upon a cyclist riding to work and through a loudspeaker allegedly "complimented" the cyclist with, "Nice bike, ******" and "I'm going to get you off the road" while they were stopped at a red light. While still near each other a few blocks down the road at another red light, the cyclist allegedly responded by knocking on the side mirror of the van and asking, "What's the deal?" Both parties then proceeded through the light with the motorist allegedly sideswiping the cyclist and causing him slight injury.

At the trial level, a Cuyahoga County jury found the motorist guilty of felonious assault, which is defined as "**knowingly** causing physical harm by means of a deadly weapon." In this case, it was the van! However, on appeal of this conviction, the 8th District Cuyahoga County Court of Appeals reversed, finding the evidence was legally insufficient to establish that the motorist "knowingly" attempted to cause the cyclist physical harm. The cyclist was sideswiped, not hit directly, and the Appeals Court noted the cyclist never fell off his bike. As obvious as it may be to some that sideswiping a person on a bike with a van is clearly dangerous, this Court determined that regardless of his purpose, the motorist's conduct failed to rise to the level of "knowingly" hurting the cyclist. The motorist's attorney successfully argued the driver didn't know sideswiping a cyclist would injure him.

This 2:1 decision again demonstrates that criminal conduct is fact driven and is another example of a decision that could have gone either way and actually resulted in a felony conviction that was overturned on appeal. Motorists should know that when they intentionally hit a cyclist, even "gently," they can be charged (and possibly convicted) of felonious assault, a conviction that can include prison time. The other valuable lesson here as a cyclist is to try to avoid escalating a confrontation like this, although this abuse was hard to ignore. The better tactic is just to stop and call the police if you are threatened.

Case type: INSURANCE COVERAGE—
INTENTIONAL ACTS
Cummings v. Lyles (Ohio Court of Appeals, 2015)[123]

The 8th District Cuyahoga County Court of Appeals held that a motorist, who pled guilty to intentionally driving into a cyclist whom he believed had stolen his son's bike, **was not covered** by his own auto liability insurance policy for the injuries he inflicted upon the cyclist.

This case illustrates a dangerous potential obstacle to **civil** (non-criminal) justice for a cyclist intentionally hit by a motorist. A motorist who **intentionally** injures someone will have no applicable liability insurance coverage available to compensate that person for their injuries. This leaves the cyclist to try to recover against the motorist's personal assets, which may be few or nonexistent. **Ohio law prohibits liability insurance covering damages caused by intentional acts; liability insurance does not exist to shield a person from intentional wrongdoing.**

In a case where a crash and injury were not intentional, liability coverage should apply. The point here is to try to remain calm in the moments after a crash and don't jump to conclusions that could negatively affect you, such as assuming the motorist hit you with intent to injure you.

That said, if it's obvious that a motorist intentionally hit a cyclist to injure them, that motorist should be prosecuted to the fullest extent of the law, and a punitive damages claim should be pursued against the wrongdoer. Once again, what you do immediately after a crash is important.

This same rationale would apply to a situation where a cyclist intentionally injures another cyclist. An irate cyclist ramming or striking another cyclist is not the proper way to resolve a dispute. If injury results and was intended, no liability insurance will cover the rammer.

Case type: WRONGFUL DEATH OF A CYCLIST
Passwaters v. Knaur (Ohio Court of Appeals, 2006)[124]

A motorist was trying to pass another motor vehicle that was following closely behind two adolescents riding their bikes. As he attempted the maneuver, he allegedly ran out of space as he approached a no passing zone while still positioned on the wrong side of the road, so he beeped his horn, presumably to get the cyclists to move out of his way or to make room in the lane to accommodate his vehicle. One of the adolescent cyclists allegedly made a sharp left movement in front of the defendant and was tragically killed. The cyclist's family brought a wrongful death negligence suit against the motorist, but the jury found the motorist wasn't negligent and this outcome was affirmed on appeal.

It's hard to know what the cyclist intended to do when he moved left, but it is unlikely he intended to put himself in danger. It seems far more likely that he was startled and simply trying to avoid the source of the horn and possibly misjudged where the sound was coming from. If a motorist sounds their horn—even with good intention—it can startle cyclists, and they might not know how, or even be able, to react. Please remember, cyclists, if someone in a motor vehicle sounds their horn while passing you on your bike, you want to try to stay to the right. If that's unsafe or not practicable, hold your line and try to remain as predictable as possible.

A cyclist moving to the left to pass or to turn left must make sure it is clear to get over and should signal that intention if the cyclist is able. A rear-view mirror or the new Garmin Radar Varia can warn you if there is a vehicle behind you when you have to merge over to the left.

Case type: CYCLIST vs. CYCLIST: MULTI-USE
TRAIL—LIABILITY
Deutsch v. Birk (Ohio Court of Appeals, 2010)[125]

An experienced cyclist riding on the multi-use Little Miami Bike Trail was severely injured when a young girl pushed her bicycle across the trail and into the path of the cyclist. The injured cyclist brought a negligence civil suit against the child to recover damages for his injuries. The Ohio 12th District Court of Appeals ruled that the child owed no duty to the injured cyclist because both were engaged in a recreational activity and "assumed the risks" inherent to the activity. Unless the child had acted in a legally reckless or willful manner, there would be no civil liability. The Court refused to apply the traffic laws applicable to bikes ridden on the road, reasoning that this was a multi-use trail including walking, jogging, skateboarding, rollerblading, and horseback riding, and the laws the injured cyclist invoked were applicable only to bicycles operated on the road, or "on paths set aside for the exclusive use of bicycles".

This case could have gone differently if it had happened on the road because pushing a bike into an oncoming vehicle (bike) already on the road would not be an inherent risk of riding a bike on the road. I also think recklessness could have been explored further. While I do not agree that riding your bike on an all purpose trail is akin to playing football or baseball where one assumes the inherent risk of the game, this is still a prime example of why cyclists who ride at higher speeds rightly have the option of riding on the road. The unpredictability and potential nonliability of other trail users, coupled with the speed differential between various trail users, offers strong justification for Ohio law providing cyclists with an absolute right to ride on the road if they so choose. This is not to say that you should refrain from riding on multi-use paths, but it is important to understand the risks of doing so and to tailor your riding and expectations accordingly.

Finally, I believe it can be reckless to enter a muti-use path in front of an oncoming cyclist without any warning or observation of what is coming down the trail, especially since it is almost impossible to avoid someone or something abruptly entering the trail while you are riding at a reasonable speed.

Case type: POLITICAL SUBDIVISION LIABILITY—
ROAD CONDITIONS
Crabtree v. Cook (Ohio Court of Appeals, 2011)[126]

In Columbus, two cyclists were riding beneath an underpass on a road that was littered with potholes and other road hazards. To avoid the hazards, one of the cyclists had to ride toward the center of the lane and was hit from behind by a speeding motorist, rendering him a quadriplegic. At the trial level, in addition to suing this motorist, the cyclist sued the City of Columbus for "negligent failure to keep public roads in repair (or) other negligent failure to remove obstructions from public roads," as required by State statute. The City raised the defense of Governmental Immunity, a legal doctrine that acts as a shield from liability for municipalities, claiming that the potholes the cyclist was avoiding were merely a "nuisance" and not an "obstruction." The Trial Court agreed with the City and dismissed the suit.

The 10th District Court of Appeals of Franklin County reversed the Trial Court's decision and held that the City of Columbus was not immune from liability because an exception to the immunity shield exists when a political subdivision negligently fails to keep roads in repair or fails to remove "obstructions" from the public roads. Unlike the Trial Court, the Court of Appeals found that potholes are not just a nuisance for cyclists and under some circumstances may also constitute an "obstruction" the City had a duty to remove.

Please note: This well-thought-out and just decision by the 10th District doesn't mean that all cyclists have a "clear road" to recover against political subdivisions, i.e., cities, counties, and townships, for road imperfections. Generally, cases against political subdivisions for road hazards are difficult and highly fact contingent. Even when an exception may exist, political subdivisions enjoy many other defenses not generally available to an individual or non-governmental entity. When in doubt, always seek the counsel of an experienced bike attorney.

Also, both private and public landowners can typically assert the defense of "recreational immunity", an Ohio statute that provides limited immunity for landowners who open their land for free to recreation activities such as cycling.[127 & 128]

Case type: PREMISE LIABILITY

Storc v. Day Drive (Ohio Court of Appeals, 2006)[129]

A cyclist sued Office Max after his bike hit a hole on the store's sidewalk at 10:30 at night, injuring the cyclist. The Trial Court dismissed the case. In a split decision, the 8th District Cuyahoga County Court of Appeals affirmed that Office Max had no liability because the hole was an "open and obvious" danger, and that the attendant circumstance of it being dark did not excuse the Plaintiff of his failure to notice the hole until it was too late. Moreover, because the cyclist failed to submit evidence proving Office Max knew (or should have known) the hole existed, they had no duty to the cyclist.

This is an excellent example of how sidewalks can be fraught with dangers for cyclists, and how business or property owners are not responsible if the cyclist can't show that the owners created, or had knowledge of the defect, or if the defect was "open and obvious." Premise negligence is a slippery fish. Also! Please remember that it's often illegal to ride on the sidewalk in a business district.

Case type: HOME RULE—OHIO REVISED
CODE (ORC) v. LOCAL ORDINANCE
Kane v. City of Dayton (Montgomery County Common Pleas Court, 2018)[130]

In Kane v. Dayton, Dayton's local ordinance relaxed Ohio law and only required bike lights to be on one hour **after** sunset. (Ohio law requires bike lights **at** sunset.) A cyclist was hit by a motor vehicle and injured within the one-hour period after sunset when he didn't have his lights on. Not having his lights on wasn't illegal under Dayton's ordinance, but it **was** illegal under the Ohio Revised Code.

The Court of Common Pleas of Montgomery County conducted a "home rule" analysis to determine which law controlled and held that the Dayton ordinance must yield to the state law. The Dayton ordinance was an exercise of police powers (not local administration) that normally belongs to the State. The ORC statute in question is a general law of Ohio designed to operate uniformly; prescribing conduct that applies to all citizens generally.

This case illustrates the importance of local ordinances following and not conflicting with state law, in this case, mandatory state law requiring lights from sunset to sunrise.

Case type: WHY YOU SHOULD NOT
REPRESENT YOURSELF!
Bailey v. Vaughn (Ohio Court of Appeals, 2017)[131]

The Eighth District Court of Appeals for Cuyahoga County established the "poster child" of why a person should not represent themselves when making a liability claim. Bailey was hit by an at fault motorist, Vaughn. Vaughn's liability insurance company orally offered Bailey $1,500 in settlement, giving up his right to "file a lawsuit or make any further claim for bodily injury" against Vaughn. Bailey orally accepted. Bailey later had a change of heart and returned the uncashed $1,500 check because his medical bills from the accident totaled $7,505!

Bailey alleged mutual mistake negated the settlement. The Court of Appeals held that there was no mutual mistake because the parties "explicitly and unambiguously" intended to release Vaughn from liability.

Interestingly, Bailey also agreed to identify and hold Vaughn harmless from any and all claims relating to this crash. What if Bailey's health insurer had a subrogation clause, and now goes to enforce it against Bailey, who might have to pay back the insurer for that coverage?!

Representing yourself for anything, except a very minor accident, is unwise. I have seen daughters and sons try to help their elderly parents through a personal injury case, doing them no favors in the end. It takes a professional to handle a personal injury case of any substance, yet some people are afraid to go to an injury attorney because they think they can't afford it. Almost all injury attorneys take their cases on a contingency basis, so no money is needed upfront or down. Yes, you may pay a rather hefty fee in the end, but it will usually result in substantially more compensation. Also, insurance companies are out to help the insurance company save money and the only way to do that is to pay less on a claim, rather than more.

Subrogation is always an issue that must be considered in an injury claim. You're not sure what subrogation really means? See what I mean?! The term "subrogation" means the right of your health insurance carrier, which paid your accident-related medical bills, to seek their money back from your settlement!

See Chapter Six for Ohio bike cases involving group riding.

14

ROAD SAFETY & CRASH STATISTICS

NATIONAL, STATE AND LOCAL

EVERY STATE IN OUR NATION is facing the issue of rising roadway deaths.

And it's happening as other wealthy nations are doing a better job of protecting vulnerable road users (VRUs) such as pedestrians and cyclists. Three foreign service officers were killed while biking or walking in the DC area in 2022, more than had died that year overseas. Dan Langenkamp, one victim's husband and a fellow foreign service officer, shared at a rally honoring his wife: "It's infuriating to me…to know that we are such failures on this issue."

Other countries are watching their traffic fatalities fall as ours continue rising. Even during the pandemic, when other countries had less motor vehicle travel and fewer deaths, U.S. deaths went **up** despite less driving! But the old story of crashes and deaths as an "unavoidable cost of mass mobility" on America roads is no longer being accepted.

Road Safety in the U.S.

Speeding motorists are more of a hazard than they have been since 2006.

In October 2021 the National Highway Traffic Safety Administration (NHTSA) reported that in the first half of 2021, deaths caused by motor vehicles had risen 18.4% since the previous year.[132] That's over 20,000 people! Additional behavioral research from the organization revealed that speeding incidents–and, not buckling up–for the period March 2020 through June 2021 were higher than before the pandemic began. Add to that a 13% increase in vehicular miles traveled from January to June 2021, and we have roadways that are even **less** calm than usual.

The U.S. Department of Transportation (USDOT) announced on January 27, 2022, its National Roadway Safety Strategy (NRSS) under the leadership of Secretary of State Pete Buttigieg, with a "long-term goal of reaching zero roadway fatalities".[133]

As part of NRSS and in recognition of the sharply increasing rate of traffic deaths for pedestrians and cyclists, USDOT is adopting a five-part "Safe System Approach". This comprehensive plan takes into account human vulnerability and error, with categories including **people** (Complete Streets initiative for communities of all sizes–"from our largest cities and towns, to rural and tribal communities all across the country"), **roads** (construction and maintenance of safer roadways), **vehicles** (safety improvements via technology, rulemaking on automatic braking, and New Car Assessment updates), **speeds** (setting limits), and **care for accident victims, post-crash**.

A portion of the Biden-Harris administration's Investment in Infrastructure and Jobs Act, aka the Bipartisan Infrastructure Law, represents a $1.2 trillion investment making possible symbiotic action across the government and USDOT, which is made up of three agencies: the National Highway Traffic Safety Administration, the Federal Motor Carrier Safety Administration, and the Federal Highway Administration. It provides infusions of funds into the Safe Streets and Roads for All program and the Highway Safety Improvement Program (HSIP), with even more directed to enhanced safety programs for truck, vehicles, and behavior.

Though a lot more work is needed, we can be thankful that serious injury and death on our roadways is finally being considered both **avoidable** and **unacceptable**.

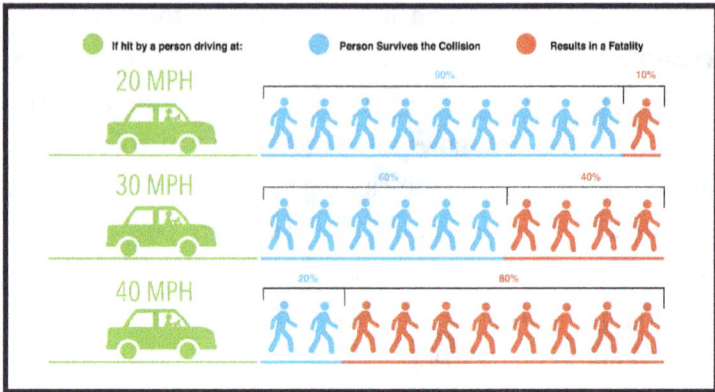

Road Safety in Ohio and Cleveland

According to a May 2021 Bike Cleveland update, fatal bike crashes across Ohio in 2020 were up 88% over the previous year.[134] This shocking percentage represents 55 individuals whose lives were cut short. In the words of Executive Director Jacob VanSickle, "It's taught us that traffic calming in the City of Cleveland can't come soon enough." After several years of preliminary activity, Bike Cleveland began its official partnership with Vision Zero Cleveland in October 2021. The overarching goal of Vision Zero Cleveland is eliminating serious injuries and deaths from crashes on Cleveland roads by 2032 through clear, measurable strategies that provide safe, healthy, and equitable mobility for all.

Current crash patterns and trends in the City of Cleveland can be found on the new Vision Zero Cleveland Data Insights page.[135]

Vision Zero Cleveland's Action Plan

In 2021 Cleveland chose the Cleveland office of NY engineering firm Nelson\Nygaard, urban design firm Seventh Hill of Cleveland and Ohio-based Bongorno Consulting to collaborate on an Action Plan. To this end, community resident feedback was sought via Citywide Engagement Events and surveys regarding the most important actions to improve roadway safety for all. Nearly 200 Cleveland residents shared their street safety concerns, the top three of which were speeding, personal safety, and distracted drivers, with cars running red lights and pedestrian safety not far behind. Requests included more crosswalks, bike infrastructure, improved general safety (guns), more security/police, traffic calming, child safety and additional crossing guards, better lighting, and improved road conditions in general. Other input revealed the desire for more road space for bikes and pedestrians, signage to encourage paying attention, additional public transportation, and community unity. Survey respondents want to increase their own walking, bicycling, and transit use, and do less motor vehicle driving.

Elements of a Safe System

Residential feedback was considered for creating a Safe System with principles to guide goals and strategies:

- Death/serious injury is unacceptable.

- Humans make mistakes.

- Humans are vulnerable.

- Responsibility is shared.

- Safety is proactive.

- Redundancy is crucial.

Elements of a Safe System include safe roads, vehicles, speeds, and people, plus post-crash care to support crash victims and their loved ones:

- Safe Roads: Prioritize safe, healthy, and equitable mobility in decision-making and capital investments; integrate safety into roadway projects; integrate safety in ongoing maintenance and operations; increase community understanding of and participation in transportation project decisions.

- Safe Vehicles: Ensure that public and private vehicles protect all road users.

- Safe Speeds: Prevent crashes from having life altering impacts by slowing speeds on Cleveland streets.

- Safe People: Increase knowledge, community support and adoption of safe practices across all road users; reform driver education to include focus on safety and multimodal knowledge. (See Chapter 22 for how the Ohio Department of

Public Safety, which oversees Driver Training, recently updated bicycle-related content in the Ohio Driver Manual.)

- Post-crash care: Support people affected by crashes; learn from crashes and post-crash site investigations to improve safety.

Other next steps include development of a neighborhood traffic calming pilot and pursuit of funding opportunities for safety improvements.

More feedback was sought at a citywide webinar in April 2022 and the opportunity continues via Vision Zero Open Houses.

State Highway Safety

Additional insight was gleaned from the 2022 Roadmap of State Highway Safety laws report by the Advocates for Highway and Auto Safety.[136] Applying a green/yellow/red rating system to 16 traffic safety laws in all U.S. states and Washington, DC, the report shows Ohio lagging in passenger safety for children, occupant protect, and–especially alarming for cyclists–impaired driving. Cyclists are innately more vulnerable than motor vehicle drivers even when motorists are completely unimpaired. Regarding the passage of safety laws designed to reduce crashes and fatalities, Ohio ranked in the bottom 11 states, and it was rated yellow for teen and distracted driving laws.

That may sound a little grim, but efforts have continued for stronger traffic safety legislation, and we finally have a breakthrough with the passing of Ohio's driving while texting law, Ohio Revised Code §4511.204[137] effective on April 4, 2023. This legislation makes driving while texting an illegal primary offense, subject to several exceptions and excluding hands-free wireless devices. Ohio also has a broad distracted driving prohibition as a secondary offense–see Chapters Three and Eight–Ohio Revised Code §4511.991.[138]

Bicycle Friendly State Report Cards

The League of American Bicyclists released 2022 Report Cards for all U.S. states. Ohio's rank is 17%, up from 18% in 2019 when the last Report Cards were created. Even better, Ohio ranks fourth out of thirteen Midwestern states![139]

15

....

E-BIKES
& OHIO LAW

MORE AND MORE, "pedal powered" or "muscle bikes"—the kind we grew up with—are competing with another type of bike—the electric bike, or e-bike. E-bikes are road legal in Ohio (except on closed access freeways) just like traditional muscle powered bikes and are the fastest-growing segment of the bike market in the United States. As of September 2018, one million e-bikes had been sold in the U.S. The cost—ranging from around $1,500 for a basic model to $10,000+ for a luxury ride—clearly isn't scaring away consumers!

Bike shops in the Greater Cleveland area and beyond stock e-bikes and/or road bikes, including but not limited to: Spin Bike Shop,[140] Gear Up Velo,[141] Beat Cycles, Century Cycles, Blazing Saddle Cycle, Eddy's Bike Shops, Joy Machines Bike Shop, All-Around Cyclery, Cycle Sport and Fitness, Bike

Authority, The Broadway Cyclery, Solon Bicycle, Bicycle Bill's (Vermilion), Marty's Bike Shop (Massillon), Ernie's Bike Shop (Massillon), Ride On Wooster, Blimp City Bike & Hike (Akron), Dirty River Bicycle Works (Akron) and it's exclusively e-bikes at Electric Pete's E-bikes in Seville.[142] As e-bikes become more popular this list will only grow, and before long we might even start seeing used e-bikes work their way into the Ohio City Bicycle Co-op's fleet of pre-owned bikes for sale. On March 22, 2022, Bird e-bikes were added to its existing fleet of e-scooters available for rent in Cleveland[143] joining Lime, which at the time of writing has well over 100 e-bikes in Cleveland and aims to double its fleet by 2023.[144]

What is an E-bike?

E-bikes are low-speed bicycles **equipped with electric motors** that run on lithium-ion batteries. Battery, controller, and motor are fully incorporated into the bike's componentry. E-bikes handle similarly to a regular bike, but they weigh more due to the motor and battery. They can still be pedaled if the battery runs out, and some classes of e-bikes are equipped with a throttle controlled by hand and don't require pedaling, while others provide an optional power boost when you turn the pedals, helping you to achieve a higher speed with less effort than you could achieve using only muscle power.

E-bike Benefits

Moving at speeds like those of regular bicycles, e-bikes allow riders to climb hills with less effort and to extend trip lengths. These factors can encourage riders to bike more frequently, increasing the frequency of bikes on the road and normalizing their presence. E-bikes also offer a new recreational option for people with physical limitations that might prevent them from enjoying traditional bikes. With additional benefits of being emission-free and low impact with relatively silent operation, e-bikes are here to stay. They may be more expensive than traditional bikes, but they're still cost-effective in comparison to motor vehicles.

E-bike Legislation by State

Since 2015 there's been considerable statewide legislative action regarding e-bikes. Some of this action focused on revising older state laws that formerly classified e-bikes as mopeds or scooters, and addressing some of the burdensome licensure, registration or equipment requirements that existed. Instead, they adopted a three-tiered e-bike classification system based on speed capabilities and method of propulsion. At the time of writing, 44 states **including Ohio** plus the District of Columbia have an **electric bicycle definition** and laws governing their operation.[145] In states that have not yet updated their laws, e-bikes aren't specifically defined and may be classified in the moped or motorized bicycle group. If you're reading this and you don't live in Ohio, check your state's law.

California has proposed licensing e-bikes! Teenagers there are dying in e-bike crashes . . .[146] Requiring a license to drive a Class 3 in Ohio may be a good idea.

E-bikes are not without controversy. It is a well-known fact that many e-bikes can be jimmied to increase the speeds listed in the class of the e-bike. Providing a vehicle that goes 20 or more miles an hour to a minor with no driver license has led to the deaths of some teenagers in California. Now the Golden State is considering licensing all e-bikes. In Ohio, at the time of writing, you do have to be 16 years old and wear a helmet to ride a class 3 e-bike, but there are no age or helmet regulations on class one and two e-bikes.

E-bikes can be very powerful, especially Class 3. Anybody who is purchasing an e-bike should check out the bike safety tips in this book and read *E-Bike Smart: Your Guide to Safe Riding*[147] from PeopleForBikes and League of American Bicyclists.

E-bikes and the Environment

PeopleForBikes endorses a first-of-its-kind e-bike battery recycling coalition which, as of this writing and thanks to the participation of 54 e-bike manufacturers, has already recycled over 36,000 pounds of lithium ion batteries.[148]

Ohio's E-bike Law

Ohio became the 11th state with an industry-supported e-bike law. Ohio House Bill 250 went into effect in March 2019, addressing requirements for electric bicycle use in Ohio and explicitly excluding e-bikes from the definition of motor vehicles.[149] Despite having a motor, e-bikes are classified as bicycles (and as such, vehicles) in Ohio. They have pedals and are usually muscle-assisted. **Like regular bikes, e-bikes don't require a license, registration, or insurance.**

Ohio's Three-Tiered E-bike Classification System

Thirteen states **including Ohio** require that a label stating classification number, top assisted speed, and motor wattage be affixed to all e-bikes.[150]

Ohio law provides that:

- A Class 1 e-bike is only pedal-assisted, has no throttle, with a maximum assisted speed of 20 mph.[151]

- A Class 2 e-bike, in addition to pedal-assisted, can also be ridden with assistance of a throttle; can maintain max speed of 20 mph.[152]

- A Class 3 e-bike is pedal-assisted, has no throttle, with 28 mph as max allowed assisted speed.[153]

Class 1 and Class 2 e-bikes are generally treated the same as traditional bicycles and are permitted on multi-use trails. Class 1 and Class 2 e-bikes may be used on the network of all purpose rails and mountain bike trails but must travel safely and with respect to other trail users. Because of their higher speeds, Class 3 e-bikes capable of 28 mph are not generally allowed in such places and are reserved for the road. Additional regulations in Ohio on Class-3 e-bikes include a bike helmet for anyone operating or riding as a passenger on a Class 3 e-bike,[154] and one must be at least 16 to operate a

Class 3 electric bicycle (a person under the age of 16 may still ride as a passenger if that Class 3 e-bike is designed to carry passengers.)[155]

Where to Ride E-bikes

Bike Cleveland has a comprehensive resource page—which you should check periodically—that covers the definitions and permissions for e-bikes.[156] Following is a reproduction of some of that information regarding where we can ride each type of e-bike at the time of writing:

- Per the Ohio Revised Code (ORC), Class 1 and Class 2 electric bicycles may ride on paths that are shared use, or exclusively set aside for bikes, unless prohibited by a resolution, ordinance, or rule passed by a controlling entity (such as a city, township, or other authority such as the Cleveland Metroparks, which is a state agency and political subdivision of Ohio).[157]

- A Class 3 electric bicycle is generally confined to the road and is allowed on a shared use path or bike path **only if the path is adjacent to a highway,** or if a controlling authority specifically granted permission.[158]

  All classes of electric bicycle are prohibited from riding on trails meant for mountain bike riders, hikers, horseback riders or similar users, unless special permission from a controlling authority has been granted.[159]

Riding in the Cleveland Metroparks

At the time of writing, all Classes of e-bikes can be ridden on the road; Class 1 and Class 2 e-bikes can be ridden on the paved multi-use trails and the mountain bike trails in the Cleveland Metroparks, but Class 3 e-bikes are prohibited on all trails.

Riding in the Cuyahoga Valley National Park (CVNP)

In accordance with Ohio law, all classes of e-bikes can be used on the roadways throughout the CVNP, but there are limits regarding trail usage. Class 1 and Class 2 e-bikes, but not Class 3, are at the time of writing allowed on all of the trails that traditional bikes are permitted on, including the Towpath. All Classes of e-bikes **are prohibited on** CVNP's **Mountain Bike Trails.** Furthermore, the current guidelines from the CVNP require e-bikes can only be used in "pedal assist" mode, not solely with the throttle.

When in doubt as to where you can legally ride, look for a sign or a park representative before rolling into uncertain territory. Better yet, research the location beforehand!

Electric Mountain Bikes

- Mountain e-bikes are always Class 1; despite what you may be seeing in mountain biking magazines, at the time of writing e-bike classes are **prohibited** from use of **mountain bike trails** in the CVNP, but Classes 1 and 2 are permitted on the Metroparks **mountain bike trails.**

- **Always** check your trails local rules for any changes.

A Final Note . . .

To really understand e-bikes, you need to ride them. During a 2022 e-bike trade show, a major bike company representative said there should be no limitations on e-bikes regardless of class. As I've shared here, however, Ohio law, bike clubs, the CVNP and the Metroparks **do** limit use based on class. Even within the classes, various nuances appear that cloud the picture and make these distinctions questionable. My crystal ball says the bike rep is probably mostly right and there will be more widespread use and fewer exclusions on e-bikes. The bottom line is, no matter what bike you ride, you have to ride with awareness and safety by following the rules of the road.

16

CYCLING SAFETY & KIDS

A STRONG FOUNDATION

WE ALL KNOW that **safety** is the most important thing when cycling, no matter what the age of the cyclist. This holds especially true for children!

Given the increase in cycling in recent years including ever-increasing infrastructure, kids in our communities should learn as early as possible about cycling safety. Bikes may start out as toys for the very young, but by the time a child is kindergarten-aged they typically have a balance bike or a bike with training wheels and an adult teaching them how to ride. Once on two wheels, the stakes are even higher. Although younger children typically ride their bikes close to home, in driveways and on neighborhood sidewalks, they will carry safety lessons forward as they, and their bikes, grow!

As mentioned in Chapter Three, the National Highway Transportation Safety Administration (NHTSA) agrees, stating in its "Bicycle Safety" publication that since young children can't always make safe decisions when riding on the road unsupervised, children under 10 are safer when cycling away from traffic.[160] Check your local ordinances to determine restrictions on children's sidewalk and road riding.

Cycling Apparel, Starting at the Top

Protecting the heads and brains of young riders couldn't be more important. This basic knowledge can be used to impress helmet usage with age-appropriate examples, e.g., our brains live in our heads; our brains help us to know our names, draw pictures, see flowers growing outside, hear our dog barking, etc. Our brains also help us ride our bikes and help us cycle safely! So, let's protect our brains.

Helmets are optional for adults in Ohio (and not all municipalities require them for cyclists under 18) but many local ordinances require them, and parents set a great example by wearing helmets and making sure their kids do, too. The risk of traumatic brain injury goes way down–as much as an 85% reduction–when our heads are protected. According to University Hospitals in collaboration with Rainbow Babies & Children's Hospital and Safe Kids Greater Cleveland, a helmet should:

- Have straps that, when fastened, form a "V" under **ears** and be a little tight, yet comfortable.

- Fasten snugly under chin; when the cyclist opens their **mouth** as wide as they can, the helmet should fit snugly on their head–if not, they should tighten the straps; another technique is making sure only one finger fits between the buckle and the chin.

- Allow for width of two fingers on forehead between brows and lower edge of helmet.

- When on, the bottom rim of the helmet should be visible to the **eyes** of the cyclist, when looking up.

- Have a U.S. Consumer Product Safety Commission (CPSC) sticker inside, indicating the helmet's performance requirements have been met.

Determining and Testing Helmet Fit

For the correct fit, the young cyclist's head can be measured approximately one inch above the eyebrows, with helmet size based on this measurement. An adult can test the fit of the cyclist's helmet by instructing the cyclist to hold their head still. The adult places their hand flat on the helmet's top and rocks it back and forth, then side to side. If the helmet fits properly, the scalp will also move. If instead the helmet slides over the scalp, a smaller helmet is needed. Watch out for helmets tipped up too high or tilted to one side.

Don't let your child tip their helmet up or sideways because it won't protect them!

Establish Best Practices Early

According to Safe Kids Worldwide, nearly 50 children per hour visit ERs with injuries related to bikes, skates, skateboards, or scooters. Among parents who claim to always wear a helmet, 86% say their child does, too. The percentage of kids wearing helmets drops to 38% among parents who say they never wear a helmet.

Build bike safety habits early. Set a great example by wearing a helmet, and consider adopting a "no helmet, no bike" rule as early as the tricycle days. This includes when a child is a passenger on an adult's bike. It also includes kids wearing helmets even if their friends do not. A simple explanation of "riding on wheels" being fun but sometimes dangerous, and that their heads need protecting, should suffice. If kids are allowed feedback during helmet shopping, they're much more likely to enthusiastically wear them, and if putting on their helmet is their own idea, it can be rewarded with a small treat or privilege. Knee and elbow pads can offer additional protection.

The League of American Bicyclists has published a Youth Skills Instructor's Manual[161] offering guidance for younger kids who are new on bikes and older kids ready to make the move from sidewalk to road riding. The book also covers organizing and facilitating clinics and bike rodeos for youth while offering key takeaways for parents and other adults.

The Brighter, the Better!

Wearing brightly colored, fluorescent clothing when cycling is a great habit to instill. Kids are naturally drawn to bright, fun colors and wearing them can only increase their visibility to others. The addition of reflective tape to their clothing down sides of shorts/pant legs, socks, and on shoes (think: moving parts) can be especially helpful once the sun begins to set. And make sure your young cyclist isn't wearing long or overly loose clothing that could get caught in wheel spokes or bike chains.

Look and Listen

With the array of electronics available today, it's important that kids know to use both their **eyes** and their **ears** to stay safer when riding their bikes. Listening to music with earbuds when riding interferes with the ability to hear important sounds around them such as larger vehicles, people walking behind and past them, other people on bikes, dogs, etc.

Also important is teaching them to keep an eye out for potential hazards ahead on the pavement as they ride–things as large as people, animals, and vehicles, and as small as gravel, litter, or holes on a sidewalk. Always teach your young riders to be on the lookout at driveways and intersections for motor vehicles pulling in and out!

17

THE JULIE NOTICE

ALERT YOUR LOCAL AUTHORITY! STORM DRAINS CAN BE DANGEROUS TO CYCLISTS

BIKE CRASHES are truly personal to me. At age 11 my sister Julie was severely injured when the front tire of her bike got caught in a sewer grate, propelling her from her bike and knocking out her front teeth. Wow! It was a tough pill for a girl that age to have to swallow!

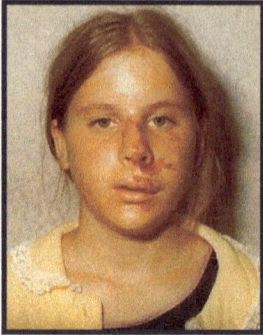

My sister Julie, and the dangerous sewer grate that
stopped her bike in its tracks

I was contacted in late 2022 by Dale Stalnaker, an avid bicyclist and a member of Lake Erie Wheelers Cycling Club and Silver Wheels Cycling Club. Dale had been encountering potential danger on club rides in Rocky River due to drainage grates with openings running parallel along Linden Road.

Dangerous grate!

Due to the parallel bar placements, a bike tire could easily become stuck in one of these grates, causing serious risk of injury to a cyclist.

The American Association of State Highway and Transportation Officials warns that drainage grates with openings running parallel to the curb can cause narrow bicycle wheels to drop into the gaps and cause a severe crash. Care must be taken to ensure drainage grates are bicycle-safe, with openings small enough to prevent a bike wheel from falling into the slots of the grate. There are several different grate styles, ones with smaller grids and narrower openings that are better and safer for bikes.[162]

The Federal Highway Administration currently recommends a few different grate designs to minimize risks for bicyclists. Bars can be perpendicular to the direction of travel or, when the bars follow the direction of travel, there can be crossbars up to six inches apart to keep wheels from getting caught. There are also designs with small shapes such as a hexagon that achieve the same safety effect.[163]

The Ohio Department of Transportation states: Shared lanes are the most common bicycle accommodations since bicycles may operate on all roadways except were prohibited by ORC Section 4511.051.[164]

Many cities in Ohio, such as Cleveland, Columbus, Cincinnati, and Westlake have changed or are changing their stormwater grates to reduce the risk to bicyclists on the road. Seeing similar hazardous grates on your rides?

On the Knabe Law Firm website[165] is a link to the Julie Notice, a customizable letter you can send to your own City officials.

I'm happy to report that Rocky River responded promptly to our communication and ordered replacement grates for installation in 2023. As of June 2023, all but one of them have been replaced! Kudos to the following officials: Safety Service Director Rich Snyder, Law Director Michael O'Shea, and Mayor Pamela E. Bobst for their quick action and willingness to make the city safer, bike friendly, and free from these preventable hazards that could cause serious injury to cyclists on roadways.

18

....

BIKE CLEVELAND

NEO'S PREMIER BICYCLE ORGANIZATION

I CANNOT OVERSTATE my admiration and appreciation of Bike Cleveland! Under the direction of Executive Director Jacob VanSickle since 2012, the Bike Cleveland team offers safe cycling education, bike infrastructure improvements, safer roads for cyclists, and bike advocacy.

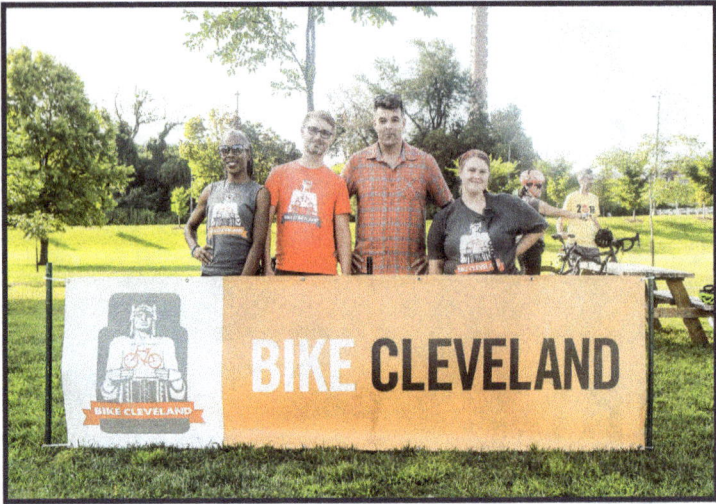

Diana Hildebrand, Jacob VanSickle, Jason Kuhn & Jenna Thomas

They guide cyclists and others concerned about safer road-ways in how they can best contribute their own time and voices. They get people working **together** for the common good of the community. As studies have shown, cycling is good for livability!

New cyclists and those wanting to know more about this great organization and its activities should check out its website.[166] In the meantime, following are some highlights in alphabetical order:

- **Advocacy Center:** Where we can take action to create safer streets for cyclists and pedestrians! Get help identifying legislators; sign up for current action alerts concerning policies and projects such as safer speed limits, stronger distracted driving laws, and Vizion Zero community events; learn about public comment periods and **make your voice heard.**

- **Better Streets Committees:** These city-wide committees have resident volunteers empowered to help improve their own neighborhoods' infrastructure with activities such as organizing bike-to-work and bike-to-school days, bringing bike education programs into the community to encourage alternate transportation, bike lane and crosswalk paint restoration, and more.

- **Bicycle Friendly Businesses:** Businesses thrive when surrounded by excellent bicycle infrastructure! And making bikes part of your company culture creates a healthier, happier atmosphere for your current crew and makes it more attractive to prospective employees. Bike Cleveland can guide you in becoming a Bicycle Friendly Business and being recognized nationally by the League of American Bicyclists.

- **Bike Cleveland Fundo:** The annual ride in August, presented by Bike Cleveland and powered by Knabe Law Firm; this urban/suburban ride is suitable for riders of all levels and abilities, is fully supported with rest stops and support vehicles, offers 10/30/60-mile routes, and starts and wraps up at the Cleveland Metroparks Edgewater Beach House at Edgewater Park. Fundo attendance increases every year, with 1,000 in 2021, 1,200 in 2022, and around 1,500 in 2023! I was honored to announce the start of the Fundo in 2022 and again in 2023:

Ken Announcing the 2022 BC Fundo

2023 BC Fundo Jersey with KLF

- **Bikes & Public Transit:** All RTA buses in Cleveland and Cuyahoga County are equipped with bike racks. Not sure how to use one? Bike Cleveland offers an instructional video[167] and RTA has step-by-step instructions on its site; also, bikes are always allowed on Rapid trains, two per car.[168] Ohio City Bike Co-Op[169] even has a demo unit outside if you want to practice before you "Rack-N-Roll"!

- **Cycling Education:** Classes for everyone, from new learners to seasoned riders wanting to feel more confident riding city streets; Bike Safety Town, Bike Rodeos, and Youth Bike Camps; custom education programs for larger groups such as businesses, schools, and organizations. Overseen by Diana Hildebrand, Education and Outreach Manager.

- **The Midway:** As previously mentioned, Bike Cleveland has been working toward Cleveland's Midway Protected Bike Network for years! Imagine 60 miles of two-directional center lane bike lanes buffered on either side by landscaping (eliminating the chance of dooring!), with a separate bike signal system, accessible to Clevelanders of all ages and bike skill levels. This world-class transportation system will safely, easily, and conveniently connect residents to their workplaces, schools, and regional treasures such as the Cleveland Metroparks.

- **NEO Families for Safe Streets (NEO FSS):** Bike Cleveland's chapter of Families for Safe Streets, a national organization formed in NYC. People who have been injured or have lost loved ones due to aggressive/distracted driving or dangerous street design can find help here. The group is dedicated to supporting survivors, ending Greater Cleveland traffic violence, and making our streets safer and more equitable by addressing legislation, street design, public attitudes, enforcement, and traffic culture.

- **Vision Zero:** Bike Cleveland has been a significant part of the Vision Zero Cleveland planning from the get-go, joining it in the quest for zero injuries and fatalities on Cleveland's roadways.

With many thanks to the Bike Cleveland staff for their hard work, enthusiasm, and dedication: Jacob VanSickle, Executive Director; Jason Kuhn, Communications and Events Manager; Diana Hildebrand, Education Outreach Manager; Jenna Thomas, Advocacy and Policy Manager; and Jerrod Amir Shakir, Community Organizer.

All cyclists, no matter how novice or how elite, should become a member of this great organization, which has the back of all cyclists in the Greater Cleveland area!

19

THE OHIO BICYCLE FEDERATION (OBF)

DECADES OF COMMITMENT

AS MENTIONED EARLIER in the book, I'm a proud Bicycle Law Board Member along with Cincinnati Attorney Steve Magas for the Ohio Bicycle Federation (OBF). Here I share background and current activities/initiatives of this fine bike organization. OBF has the ear of our state representatives in Columbus.

Since its founding in 1980, OBF has been Ohio's only statewide advocacy bicyclist organization, with groups and individuals working together to promote cycling for transportation, safety legislation, recreation, and more. Current (at time of writing) Ohio Bicycle Federation Chair Chuck

Smith has been working in this role since 1995. Talk about dedication!

OBF Chair Chuck Smith (left) observes former Governor Taft signing Ohio House Bill 389 (Better Bicycling in Ohio bill) on June 17, 2006

A complete historical timeline of OBF's dedicated work and accomplishments can be found on its website[170] but following are some of its many highlights:

- In 1996, OBF was instrumental in the passage of Ohio House Bill 461 which allows cyclists to point in the direction they are intending to turn (previously, a right turn had to be signaled with an upraised left arm).

- From 1997-2003 on the National Committee for Uniform Traffic Laws and Ordinances (NCUTLO), Smith represented cycling, the mission being to update the

Uniform Vehicle Code due to the definition of "bicycle" being upgraded to "vehicle".

- In 2004 OBF testified before the Ohio House and Senate Transportation Committees supporting House Bill 406, which was signed into law that year, making the "Share the Road" license plate available.

- 2005 saw the passage of House Bill 389 "The Better Ohio Cycling Bill" after OBF once again testified before the two committees; all local jurisdictions were now required to follow Ohio law about cycling, plus it made the Ohio Revised Code (ORC) closer to the Uniform Vehicle Code (UVC).

OBF Board Members at 2011 OBF display at the Ohio Transportation Engineering Conference (OTEC)
L-R: Andy Davis, Tricia Kovacs, Chuck Smith

- After eight years of educating the Ohio General Assembly, OBF testified in 2015 before the House Transportation Committee in support of House Bill 154 and again in 2016 before the Senate Transportation Committee; it was signed into law in December 2016 and included the Three Feet Safe Distance requirement when passing cyclists, and the "dead red" exception, both covered in Chapter Three.

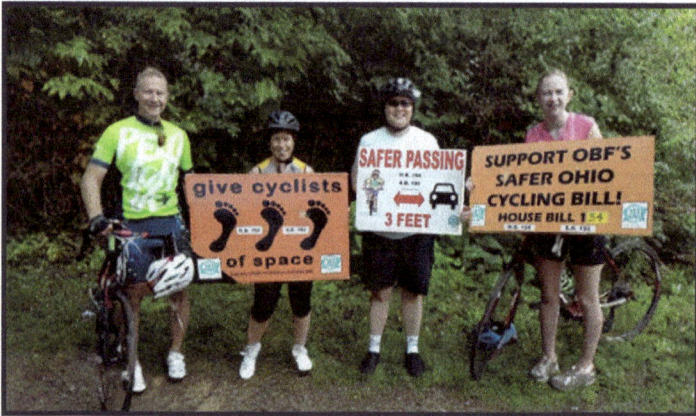

Unidentified bicyclists rally behind OBF's 3 Feet Passing Bill at Dayton Cycling Club's 2015 Wright Wride

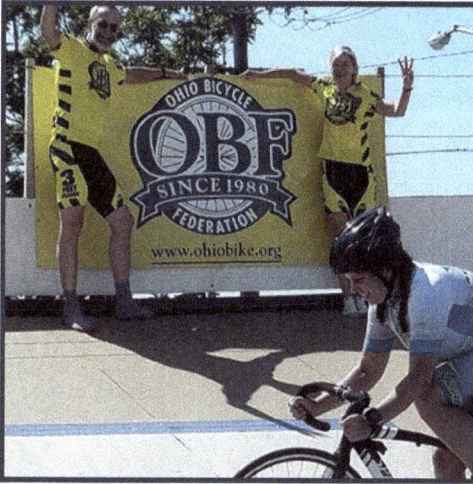

OBF Chair Chuck Smith and member of Cleveland racing team model OBF
3 Feet Passing kits designed to educate Ohio motorists concerning OBF's
3 Foot Passing Law; kits are available on OBF website at ohiobike.org
Photo taken in Cleveland Velodrome, funded in part by OBF

OBF Board Members sporting OBF 3 Feet Passing cycling kits during
the August 2022 Cycle Con in Dayton, L-R: Ken Braswell, Chuck Smith,
Ken Mercurio

- In 2020 OBF was selected by the new Ohio Traffic Safety Council to represent Ohio cycling; the same year, Smith was selected as a League of American Bicyclists Board Member.

OBF Chair Chuck Smith with ODOT Director Jack Marchbanks at OBF display during 2022 Ohio Transportation Engineering Conference (OTEC)

- OBF's years of effort and recent testifying before Ohio legislators were instrumental in the passing of Ohio Revised Code §4511.204 on April 4, 2023, **making driving while texting a primary offense!**

- As of this writing, there is discussion about developing and advocating for a Traffic Victim Support Act; Sharon Montgomery, whose husband John was killed while riding his bike by a distracted driver and who, for over two decades has worked toward making distracted driving a primary offense in Ohio, would support such legislation.

- OBF publishes the annual Ohio Bicycle Events Calendar, which includes tours (noncompetitive group rides), budget tours, free rides, full-service tours, fundraisers, bike-a-thons/pledge rides. Some years include bicycle races.

Much gratitude to the Ohio Bicycle Federation and Chuck Smith for their decades of commitment to safe cycling across our state!

20

THE OHIO TO
ERIE TRAIL

FUN AND ADVENTURE

LOOKING FOR ADVENTURE? Looking for cama-
raderie? Looking for an epic, multifaceted, fun bike trip?

Ride across Ohio–including through its three major cities–on the Ohio to Erie Trail (OTET)![171] An international cycling destination, the OTET is affectionally known as Ohio's
Crown Jewel and is rated by many cyclists as the number two
cycling experience in the country. You can start in Cleveland
with destination Cincinnati. Ride through Akron, Mill-
ersburg, Columbus, Yellow Springs or Xenia, and the Little
Miami Valley, wrapping it up in Cinci. **Or** start in Cinci and
finish in the CLE. You can do it in three days (Elite), four days

(All Pro), five days (First Team), or six-ten days (Made the Team!). (Please note, these are my unofficial labels.)

Time is greatly dependent on what you carry (or don't carry) and where and how you stay (hotel vs. glamping vs. camping). One stat that is for sure: your brain will never forget the ride!

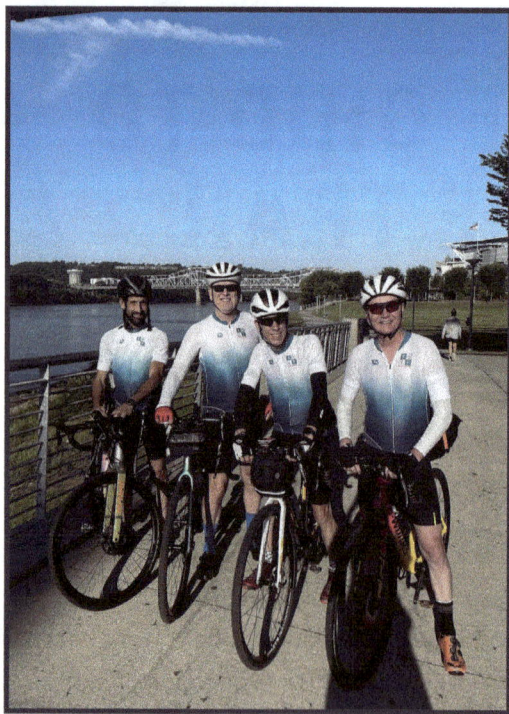

Mark Looney, Ken Knabe, Tim Furey, and Mark Davis on the OTET in Cincinnati en route to Cleveland, 2022

I'm a Board Member of the OTET[172] a unified network of contiguous multi-use greenways and trails consisting of 326 miles of mostly hard, flat surface; 290 miles of recreational trail with only 35 of its miles on city streets and rural roads–89.1% is dedicated trail as of October 2022. Also known as Ohio Bike Route 1, it is the gateway to many of the state's other contiguous trails. The OTET winds through some of the most scenic parts of our heartland. Along the OTET corridor history buffs can learn about Ohio's part in the Revolutionary and Civil Wars, the beginnings of the railroad and canal, and how the Amish first made our state home.

Founder Ed Honton was the non-profit OTET's first president. He had an idea in 1991 to create a path mostly by making use of former canal and railroad corridors. His vision is now a reality and his proud legacy lives on. Many celebrate it by becoming members of the "326 Club" when they've completed the entire 326-mile ride in a single trip. This major accomplishment can be shared with the world via a 326 Sticker, available for order on the organization's website and free with any other purchase in the OTET store.[173]

As of this writing there's also a "Trail Enthusiasts" peer-to-peer group on Facebook which can help with route assistance and navigation while you're on the trail.[174] The Trip Planning page[175] is extremely comprehensive with links to every resource you could think of, including a paper trail guide, services directory, list of campsites, lodging, shuttle, attractions, amenities/bike shops, distance planner, logo shirts, trail alerts, streets and roads guide, annual tours page, parking ideas, and of course, the 326 Club! Be sure to check out the interactive map[176] and GPS navigation files for northbound and southbound trips.[177] During the 2023 riding season, the OTET interactive map was viewed 338,000 times for an average of 1,580 views per day!

With thanks to Executive Director Jody Dzuranin, long-time former Executive Coordinator Lisa Daris, members of the Advisory Board, long-time Immediate Past President Mike Groeber,[178] current President Tom Bilcze and fellow OTET Board of Directors members[179] including the great Bob Niedenthal, creator of the aforementioned interactive map and downloadable navigation links covering all four OTET regions. Northbound and southbound printed trail guides can be purchased on the OTET website.

Cleveland is now easily passable since the Center Street Bridge repair has been completed. The Center Street Bridge offers a pivotal (pun intended!) connection of the Cleveland Centennial bike trail to Wendy Park via the Willow Avenue Lift Bridge.

The Willow Avenue Bridge is not conducive to cyclists riding recumbent bikes, due to a very narrow bike passageway; it will someday be repaired (or replaced) to allow easier passage by bike. Franklin Boulevard west from the Flats to West 25th Street and Irishtown Bend are down until 2025. Once Irishtown Bend is completed it will also allow a direct passageway to Wendy Park.

As someone who has traversed the Ohio to Erie Trail in both directions, I can attest to the sense of accomplishment that comes when you dip your tire in Lake Erie and the Ohio River. I highly recommend it as a great way to see a lot of our state–including bridges, canals, railroad and canal history, rivers, unique towns, and even horses pulling buggies–while bonding with cycling friends on a ride that's not just a journey, but a real adventure!

21

....

LOCAL NEO BIKE CLUBS

WEEKLY AND SIGNATURE RIDES

NORTHEAST OHIO has an abundance of bike clubs hosting weekly and signature rides throughout the cycling season for most levels and interests. Specific info can be found at each club's website linked in the Bibliography. The following entries feature road bike rides.

Akron Bicycle Club[180]

"ABC" also stands for this Akron-based bike club's **Absolutely Beautiful Country Ride**, which the club has been enjoying in July for over five decades! Four mileage options for rides through "the rolling hills and quaint villages of Summit,

Medina, and Wayne counties" introduce riders to safe, pictur-esque, and challenging cycling. ABC hosts the **Think Spring** ride in April and the two-day **Roscoe Ramble** in September, a tour through Amish Country farmland from Canal Fulton to Roscoe overnighting in Coshocton, then back to Canal Fulton. This ride is better suited for experienced, conditioned riders but a shorter option is available. I've had the pleasure of presenting to ABC on cycling safety and riding with them. It's a very welcoming group!

Cleveland Touring Club[181]

Mentor-based CTC's members ride with hundreds of cy-clists through Northeast Ohio's bucolic Amish countryside in Geauga County during their annual **Sunday in June** ride. The ride is based at and kicks off from Burton's historic Century Village which offers 22 buildings of local history including an authentic settlement, a collection of Civil War memorabilia, and a museum store. CTC's **Winery & Covered Bridge Tour** signature ride happens each September. With four mileage options you can visit covered bridges, lots of "rolling terrain and river valley climbs", and even some rideable gravel on one of the bridge routes.

I've enjoyed doing presentations for CTC and joining them for rides. Their commitment to safety is much appreciated!

Cleveland Critical Mass

Cleveland Critical Mass rolls out of Public Square in down-town Cleveland at 7 p.m. one Friday each month, year-round to explore a variety of routes through the city. Post-ride there is more fun to be had at a local establishment. Over 300 cities globally enjoy Critical Mass rides!

Hudson Velo Club[182]

Hudson Velo rides twice weekly. April through September, their Wednesday **Burger and Beer** ride rolls out at 6 p.m. from behind the library in downtown Hudson. The **Burton Breakfast Ride** with three mileage options is the club's signature ride in September, and the season wraps up with October's **Biketoberfest**.

Lake Erie Wheelers[183]

The Lake Erie Wheelers is a west side bike club which meets in Lakewood and is well known for hosting one of the first big road bike rides of the year–the **Chili March Metric Ride** with full metric (62 mile) and half metric (31 mile) options. The 2024 CMMR, now called the Chili Spring Metric, will be held in April, with a new starting point. This club also rides three times a week. I've enjoyed presenting to the Wheelers and riding in the Chili March Metric!

Lorain County Bicycle Club (formerly Lorain Wheelmen)[184]

LCBC rides four times weekly on average, and some members ride year-round. The club culture even offers a unique twist on the halfway point during rides–stopping to refuel at a local family restaurant! Their signature rides include April's **AFROST: A Freebie Ride and Ohio Spring Tour**; although there aren't rest stops or SAG on this one, the club does pro-vide maps and three distance (25, 51, and 57 mile) cut-offs, and there are places along the route to shop for snacks. Sup-ported rides are **Jerry's Jeromesville Journey** in May, and the **Red Flannel Metric Century**, a late fall tradition in No-vember and typically the last big road bike ride of the season listed on OBF's Cycling Calendar. Featuring three options–64 or 32 miles and a newer 24-mile Flatlanders route–the ride begins in Oberlin and is also known for its tasty chilis and other delicacies.

Silver Wheels Cycling Club[185]

Since 1998 Vermilion-based Silver Wheels has promoted both the social and technical sides of cycling while educating people in its area, becoming a 501 C(7) non-profit organiza-tion in 2002. Members include teenagers through 80-some-things hailing from Lorain County and seven other counties in NEO. The club offers over 600 events annually, mostly rides but also educational programs, regular meetings, and non-cy-cling recreation. Members hike and cross-country ski togeth-er during the off-season. The club's annual **Dog Days Wine Tour** is held in July, with major bragging rights via *Bicycling Magazine* which listed "The Dog" as "One cool ride"! Silver Wheels Cycling Club has also received the Regional Club of the Year award from the League of American Bicyclists. It is always a pleasure presenting to the members of Silver Wheels!

Slow Roll Cleveland[186]

Slow Roll Cleveland got its official **501(c)(3)** **non-profit** organization designation thanks in no small part to Aubrey Welbers, former President of the Board. Her dedication also led to Slow Roll Cleveland's being a fully insured ride, as well as partnering with city-wide organizations including Metro-Health. Longtime Slow Roller Kevin Jones stepped into the role of President of the Board in 2021. SQUAD, Slow Roll's dedicated volunteer group, has opportunities on- and off-ride including route scouting, SAG, fund-raising, and more. The Kickoff Ride and Annual Meeting is held mid-May, followed by casual rides most Monday evenings through the end of October. I was honored to donate to Slow Roll Cleveland a quantity of laminated bike cards detailing Ohio laws applicable to cyclists, with steps to take in case of a bike crash on the reverse side of the cards.

Stark County Bike Club[187]

Canton-based, non-profit Stark County Bike Club (SCBC) has been offering a robust schedule of on-road, trail, and Towpath rides since 1968. The club is big on community volunteering with a strong focus on kids' cycling and safety. SCBC is rightly proud of its status as the first organization in Ohio to help keep our roadways cleaner and more beautiful under the State's Adopt-A-Highway initiative! I have enjoyed presenting on safe cycling to this great club in conjunction with Ernie's Bicycle Shops.

22

WORKING ON
BIKE SAFETY

NATIONALLY, STATEWIDE, LOCALLY

AS AN ATTORNEY a significant part of my job includes assessing risk, and I have frequent contact with people who find themselves on the wrong side of a bad situation through no fault of their own. I'm conscious that this book discusses crashes and the dangers of cycling, but I'm also aware that many people throughout the nation are working on bike safety and things continue to head in the right direction. The following is an update on some initiatives being pursued at the federal, state, and local levels.

FEDERAL ACTION

Electric Bicycle Incentive Kickstart for the Environment Act (E-BIKE) Act

Reintroduced on March 21, 2023, the E-BIKE Act would offer consumers a 30 percent federal tax credit of up to $1,500 on the purchase of new e-bikes. The bill is endorsed by the League of American Bicyclists, PeopleForBikes, Sierra Club and numerous other organizations, and sponsors include U.S. Representatives Jimmy Panetta (CA-19), Congressional Bike Caucus Chairman and Founder Earl Blumenauer (OR-03), Mike Thompson (CA-04), and Adam Schiff (CA-30). Companion legislation has been introduced in the Senate by Senator Brian Schatz (D-HI).[188] If passed, the E-BIKE Act will offer a powerful trifecta of reduced motor vehicle trips and commute times, improved quality of life, and lower carbon emissions resulting in cleaner air and better health—burning more calories and fewer fossil fuels.

The Infrastructure Investment and Jobs Act (Bipartisan Infrastructure Bill)

This bill, originally called the INVEST in America Act (H.R. 3684), was signed into law on November 15, 2021, by President Joe Biden. The League of American Bicyclists believes this amended Act includes *"unprecedented levels of funding for active transportation and the safety of vulnerable road users, and it represents an important step towards building more livable communities".*

America's Outdoor Recreation Act of 2022

I can't wait for the day I ride from Cleveland to the East and West Coasts on my bicycle! On March 16, 2023, following up on America's Outdoor Recreation Act of 2022 in the 117th Congress, America's Outdoor Recreation Act of 2023 (AORA) was introduced in the 118th Congress by U.S. Senators Joe Manchin (D-WV) and John Barrasso (R-WY).[189] This bipartisan legislation would improve infrastructure and drive economic growth in rural areas while creating and improving the nation's outdoor recreation opportunities.

E-bike Safety Program in the Works

The League of American Bicyclists, PeopleForBikes, and Bicycle Colorado are working in tandem (pun intended!) on a first-of-its-kind e-bike rider safety curriculum to teach all riders e-bike specific best practices via steps that are clear and actionable. Centered around the League's Smart Cycling program, the free online training will offer an overview of the three classes of e-bikes. It will cover topics such as responsible e-bike ownership, preparing for your first ride, battery safety, and correct storage as well as how to position one's e-bike on the roadway, share a trail, ride predictably, and other issues so people can learn to ride their e-bikes with confidence, **safely**. The program was expected to roll out by late summer 2023.

STATE AND LOCAL ACTION

Driving While Texting

Effective April 4, 2023, Ohio Revised Code §4511.204 makes driving while texting a primary offense. This important legislation has been a long time coming and gives law enforcement officials the power to immediately pull over a driver when witnessing them texting while holding a cell phone in violation of the new distracted driving law. However, numerous exceptions exist, including (but not limited to) that a driver can still legally hold their cell phone when parked or stopped at a red light; they can still swipe to answer a call and can still use hands-free wireless devices.[190]

We cyclists know we're safer when using the right equipment, following state law regarding bike lights at night, and riding correctly. Yet other factors come into play. Motorists also must do their part for safer roadways. Unfortunately, it's impossible to keep every single motorist from driving under the influence, or—as detailed in Chapter Eight, equally as dangerous—driving while distracted. As cyclists we need to go the extra mile(s) and demand action, prioritizing safety over speed, from the following entities:

- **Auto manufacturers.** They must be urged to add available cyclist-detecting technology along with technology that will employ automatic emergency brakes, and to include systems that will monitor for intoxicated drivers.

- **Transportation departments and road commissions.** Our current roadways were designed so motor vehicles can reach their destinations as quickly as possible, yet this puts all other road users in greater danger; modern road design priorities must include safety and multi-modality, and an end to dangerous street design.

- **Our legislators.** Bipartisan bills that will keep cyclists safer should be passed and not left to flounder in our House and Senate! As constituents we are free to communicate with our legislators on these crucial issues. The squeaky wheels get the grease!

Ohio Driver Manual Updated Bike Content

The Ohio Department of Public Safety, which oversees Driver Training, recently updated the Ohio Driver Manual (Digest of Motor Vehicle Laws)–and specifically, the bicycle-related content! Notably, the following edits were made:

1. In the "Passing" section, it states, "Crossing the center line is permitted only to turn left into driveways or pass a slow-moving vehicle (e.g., bicycle or vehicle displaying a slow-moving vehicle sign)." Additionally, a large graphic was added to the bicycle section to emphasize allowing three feet of clearance when passing a bicycle.

Removal of this sentence: *Bicyclists must keep to the right edge of the roadway, allowing faster traffic to safely pass.* Instead, it addresses that bicyclists must obey traffic signs, signals, and pavement markings, and that they must follow the same rules of the road as a motorist.

Safe Routes to School

Since July 2015 the Cleveland Metropolitan School District has had the Safes Routes to School program in place. With the greater safety and health of Cleveland's children in grades K-8 in mind and established by the U.S. Department of Transportation (USDOT), early planning included representatives from ODOT, the City of Cleveland, area police departments, medical facilities and foundations, and Bike Cleveland. The Safe Routes to School program was designed to make safer the routes children take to and from school, thus reducing the number of motor vehicles dropping off and picking up and helping parents be more comfortable with their kids walking and biking to school. This has the added benefit of building physical activity into the everyday movements of kids in our community, which will help them enjoy longer, healthier lives. Safe Routes to School uses the "five Es" to make routes to school safer: Education, Encouragement, Engineering, Enforcement, and Evaluation.

This comprehensive approach has achieved such unorthodox successes as adding bicycle skills and education classes to the 3rd grade P.E. The Cleveland Safe Routes to School team is planning for route improvements in the coming years and select schools in the district are holding Walk and Bike to School Days and other events in 2023. The Cleveland Metropolitan School District continues this program locally with the support of NOACA, the City of Cleveland, ODOT, and Bike Cleveland.[191]

Calley Mersmann was there from the beginning as the Cleveland Metropolitan School District Safe Routes to School Coordinator before taking on the role of Bicycle and Pedestrian Coordinator in 2018 and playing a pivotal role in the advancement of Vison Zero Cleveland.

Cuyahoga Greenways

Known as "Cuyahoga Greenways" today, this effort began in 2014 as the "Trails Leadership Network" and consists of many stakeholders. Cuyahoga Greenways represents continued collaboration toward achieving an extensive and comprehensive system of trails, bikeways, and pedestrian routes across Cuyahoga County. The goal is to ultimately build and connect a network of trails, paths, and on-street facilities so people throughout the county can access safe and inviting recreational opportunities and active transportation. As of this writing there are twelve agencies and organizations in the collective Cuyahoga Greenway Partners (CGP)—including Bike Cleveland, Cleveland City Planning Commission, and NOACA—actively collaborating on the Greenways Plan trail and bikeway projects.

Since much of this network already exists, the focus is on identifying the missing links making it difficult to get around by bike or on foot. This is a visionary project with a long lifespan and if achieved, it will bring long-lasting benefits to the region as people increasingly choose where they live based on these kinds of amenities. People don't want to drive. They want to bike, and this will help them do it. As mentioned in the Foreword, Cleveland's Opportunity Corridor featuring a multi-use path for pedestrians and cyclists along its entire length is, as of this writing, the most recent addition to the Cuyahoga Greenways Network.

Complete and Green Streets Initiative (CGS)

The term "Complete Streets" as used in urban planning, transportation advocacy, and roadway and traffic engineering refers to streets that do more than merely funnel motor vehicles through; it also focuses on improved safety, health, and economic outcomes. Complete Streets places significant emphasis on safe access for **all** users—including pedestrians, cyclists, people making deliveries, and those riding public transportation.

Varying design elements come into play in the makeup of Complete Streets depending on the need. These elements can include median crossing islands, curb extensions, the elimination of free-flow right-turn lanes, angled parking that faces outward, and curb corner radii that is shorter (all of which help to calm traffic), and yes, specific accommodations such as protected/dedicated lanes for bikes. The "Green" in CGS comes into play via trees and other landscaping elements, recycled materials, and sustainable techniques for storm water management, working in tandem for enhanced environmental outcomes.

The City of Cleveland has had Complete and Green Streets legislation on its books since 2012, and it calls for considering a wide array of issues whenever a road is repaired. Critics contend that this was applied inconsistently—with Cleveland not always living up to its own legislation—and have been calling for better oversight and more robust CGS legislation. These calls have been answered with the City updating its CGS ordinance as part of its more comprehensive work on Vision Zero Cleveland, and safety advocates hope that this new iteration will bring more uniform change in a way that the 2012 legislation was unable to do.[192] An amended Complete & Green Streets Ordinance was introduced at Cleveland City Council on April 21, 2022. In addition to a new process of incorporating design elements for enhanced multimodal use is the creation of a 10-person Transportation Infrastructure Advisory Committee (TIAC) with four members appointed by the mayor and six by City Council. The 2022 Ordinance is multifaceted:

- City staff will offer input to the TIAC during earliest stages of project planning before funding is sought.

- Along with staff, the TIAC will provide recommendations to the Director of the Mayor's Office of Capital Projects to inform project decisions.

- Re. accountability, the public will be informed of "exceptions" in how the final project scope differs from said recommendations.

- The City will have the TIAC's assistance in evaluation of City-sponsored roadway projects.

- The City will provide an annual CGS progress report evaluating the policy's effectiveness.

- The Cleveland City Planning Commission will begin an Active Transportation Plan process for updating the 2007 Bikeway Master Plan and the 2014 Bikeway Implementation Plan.[193]

Ohio Bicycle Infrastructure/ Protected Bike Lanes

Bike lane mileage in Cleveland is up, and the city now has several protected bike lanes. The Northeast Ohio Areawide Coordinating Agency (NOACA)[194] allocated funds for upcoming projects and helped create the city's first protected bike lane. And in early 2023, plans for The Midway—Cleveland's Protected Bikeway Network[195] gained the approval of a Cleveland City Council committee.[196] The ultimate Midway vision is a "bicycle highway" system making the most of underutilized roads once used by streetcars and designed to carry a far greater motor vehicle load than is asked of them today. When complete, The Midway will extend for more than 50 miles in all directions throughout Cleveland.

As of this writing, the section known as the Superior Midway would include a 2.5-mile route down the center of Superior Avenue and running from Public Square to East 55th Street, separated from traffic and including eight-foot-wide buffers on either side of a 10-foot-wide bikeway. The Lorain Midway running from West 20th to West 65th Street would be integrated into The Midway network, helping to better connect people to a historic shopping district and hopefully, boost the local economy.

Bike Cleveland's Executive Director Jacob VanSickle—
who has been pouring his energy and effort into The Midway
project for years—believes that once these projects are completed, they will " . . . put Cleveland on the route to a network
of **world-class** sustainable transportation infrastructure."
And in the words of Mayor Justin M. Bibb, these projects will
make Cleveland "one of the best bike-friendly cities in the
country"!

With full council approval, these projects in combination
with part of the planned Lorain-Carnegie Bridge Memorial
Bridges Loop trail[197] would give cyclists riding east-west a
protected corridor "throughout the heart of the city". It could
also be the first manifestation of Cleveland's Complete and
Green Streets ordinance[198] spearheaded by Mayor Bibb and
Councilman Kerry McCormack and passed in summer 2022.

Ohio considered taking away local cities' control in
building bike lanes. Not surprisingly, the biking community
strongly protested! This time, after hearing from bike clubs
such as the Lake Erie Wheelers along with a very strong
response from Bike Cleveland as well as the early 2023 tes-
timony of Grace Gallucci, executive director of Northeast
Ohio Areawide Coordinating Agency (NOACA), State Rep.
Tom Patton (R-Strongsville) reconsidered his amendment
and removed it from the Ohio budget. As of this writing the
Superior Midway project continues in the design phase.[199]

Vision Zero Legislation and Cleveland's Side Guard Initiative

As previously mentioned in Chapter 14, Cleveland officials have moved forward with Vision Zero. The overarching goal is Vision Zero Cleveland eliminating serious injuries and deaths from crashes on Cleveland roads by 2032 through clear, measurable strategies that provide safe, healthy, and equitable mobility for all.

The City takes pedestrian and bike crashes seriously and is using data and intelligent planning principals to help reach this goal, actively addressing high crash corridors through its Vision Zero and "Complete & Green Streets" legislation. Following up on Bike Cleveland's past collaboration with the now defunct Vision Zero Task Force Data and Evaluation Subcommittee, the VZ Cleveland website offers analysis via its Crash Maps & Data section on serious injuries and fatalities, including a high injury network map.[200]

I'm an original member of Cleveland's former Vision Zero Taskforce along with Truck Safety attorney Andrew Young of The Law Firm for Truck Safety LLP.[201] Andy and I focused on lateral safety devices known as "side guards" which are installed on the sides of large commercial trucks between the front and rear wheels. In a commercial truck crash involving a cyclist or pedestrian, it's not the initial impact that typically kills or maims, but when the cyclist or pedestrian is pulled under the truck through the exposed area or gap on the side between the wheels, and then run over by the larger rear wheels in a horrible situation known as "underride". Andy donated 15 side guards which have been added to City of

Cleveland waste collection trucks. He is now working with the Ohio Bicycle Federation in Columbus to help facilitate the side guard remedy to these avoidable crashes.

The City of Cleveland and attorney Andy Young deserve credit for initiating the side guard program and meaningfully pursuing Vision Zero goals, with additional credit for recognizing the need to clarify and expand its Complete & Green Streets ordinances with input from Cleveland's Vision Zero Taskforce. The Cleveland Vision Zero Taskforce was comprised of five subcommittees and experienced significant growth since its inception in early 2018.

Vision Zero Cleveland,[202] initiated by the City of Cleveland under Mayor Justin M. Bibb and the Cleveland City Council, partners with local community groups and agencies.

Calley Mersmann, as of this writing Cleveland's Senior Strategist, Transit and Mobility shared that the City is working on integrating VZ action plan recommendations into day-to-day City operations and capital projects, onboarding additional staff to increase the capacity to implement mobility initiatives—including Vision Zero—and applying for supplemental safety funding from ODOT and USDOT to make local dollars go further. Cleveland has also concluded a successful neighborhood speed table pilot and allocated $3.5 million in ARPA funding to speed table expansion across the city and other safety/mobility improvements.

A FINAL NOTE FROM THE AUTHOR...

My VISON for this second edition is clear.

First, to educate the public on cyclists' rights and responsibilities. Sources addressing these topics are few and far between.

Second, to reiterate that we cyclists have rights and equal access to the road.[203]

Third, to stress that cyclists are not protected by 2,000 pounds of metal! A bike crash usually results in far more severe injuries than a car crash. We must band together bike advocacy organizations such as Bike Cleveland and the Ohio Bicycle Federation, bike clubs and bike shops to tweak, change, and create legislation that protects us and holds drivers that injure us to a standard commensurate with the risk. We cyclists represent every member of society and are at risk every time we're out on the road. Drivers need to know that and respect our rights.

Ultimately, motorist education, awareness, and understanding concerning cyclist rights and their vulnerability on the road are some of the most important and effective ways to reduce the number of crashes. Cyclists should know their rights **and** their responsibilities as well, but the onus should really be on motorists given the lopsided nature of vulnerability between cyclists and motorists. Practicing Vehicular Cycling can help to decrease friction and crashes when better infrastructure is lacking, but "Share the Road" cannot be mere verbiage; it must have teeth in the form of **legal consequences** for motorists failing to heed this adage. At the end of the day, we're dealing with life and limb out there. Motorists: Slow down, calm down, and remember that cyclists are co-equal users of our roadways worthy of respect.

Let's all continue the conversation!

BIBLIOGRAPHY

CITED WEBSITES and other sources current at time of writing.

As it becomes available, updates and other information regarding legislation, cycling laws, and more will be found at:

https://klfohio.com/cycling-rights-book/

1.   Cleveland Clinic/VeloSano, Home page. Accessed June 6, 2023. https://www.velosano.org/home

2.   Ohio to Erie Trail Fund, Home page. Accessed June 6, 2023. http://ohiotoerietrail.org/

3.   Wahoo Fitness, Bike Trainer page. Accessed June 6, 2023. https://www.wahoofitness.com/devices/bike-trainers/view-all

4.   Vision Zero Cleveland, Home page. Accessed June 6, 2023. https://www.visionzerocle.org/

5.   "Current Bicycle Friendly Businesses Through Summer 2022." The League of American Bicyclists. Accessed June 6, 2023. https://bikeleague.org/sites/default/files/BFB_Full_List_through_Summer_2022.pdf

6.   Bike Cleveland, Home page. Accessed June 6, 2023. https://www.bikecleveland.org/

7.   Ohio Bicycle Federation, Home page. Accessed June 6, 2023. http://www.ohiobike.org/

8.   Ohio to Erie Trail, Home page. Accessed January 9, 2023. https://www.ohiotoerietrail.org/

9.   Murnane, Kevin. "New Research Indicates Cycling To Work Has Extraordinary Health Benefits." *Forbes.* April 25, 2017. https://www.forbes.com/sites/kevinmurnane/2017/04/25/new-research-indicates-cycling-to-work-has-extraordinary-health-benefits/?sh=3b332d723e62

10.   Hunt, Lindsey. "Biking for Your Brain: The Neurology of Cycling." DuVine. Accessed June 6, 2023. https://www.duvine.com/blog/brain-biking-the-neurology-of-cycling/

11.   "Environmental Benefits of Bicycling and Walking in the United States." National Academies Transportation Research Board. Accessed June 6, 2023. https://onlinepubs.trb.org/Onlinepubs/trr/1993/1405/1405-002.pdf

12.   "How Riding a Bike Benefits the Environment." UCLA. Accessed June 6, 2023. https://transportation.ucla.edu/blog/how-riding-bike-benefits-environment#:~:text=No%20Gas%2C%20No%20Pollution,14%20million%20tons%20of%20CO2

13.   "The Environmental Benefits Of Bicycling And Walking." U.S. Department of Transportation Federal Highway Ad-

ministration. Accessed June 6, 2023. https://safety.fhwa.dot.gov/ped_bike/docs/case15.pdf

14. "The Paris Agreement," United Nations Climate Change. Accessed June 6, 2023. https://unfccc.int/process-and-meetings/the-paris-agreement/the-paris-agreement

15. "U.S. greenhouse gas emissions jumped 6.2% in 2021." *Reuters.* Accessed January 10, 2022. https://www.reuters.com/markets/commodities/us-greenhouse-gas-emissions-jumped-62-2021-report-2022-01-10/#:~:text=U.S.%20greenhouse%20gas%20emissions%20were,Rhodium%20Group%2C%20a%20research%20organization

16. Lee, Juhohn. "135 million Americans are breathing unhealthy air, American Lung Association says." CNBC, updated June 2, 2021. https://www.cnbc.com/2021/04/22/heres-how-many-americans-are-effected-by-air-pollution-every-year.html

17. Conrow, Lindsey and Mooney, Siân and Wentz, Elizabeth A. "The association between residential housing prices, bicycle infrastructure and ridership volumes." Arizona State University. Accessed June 6, 2023. https://asu.pure.elsevier.com/en/publications/the-association-between-residential-housing-prices-bicycle-infras

18. Rose, Cedric. "Cincinnati Might Actually Become A Bike-Friendly Region After All." *Cincinnati Magazine.* July 2, 2021. https://www.cincinnatimagazine.com/article/cincinnati-might-actually-become-a-bike-friendly-region-after-all/

19. Annis, Robert. "This Montana Senator Wants to Tax Every Cyclist Who Visits the State." *Bicycling.* April 4, 2017. https://www.bicycling.com/news/a20031401/this-montana-senator-wants-to-tax-every-cyclist-who-visits-the-state

20. Evans, Maxwell. "Big Marsh Park's New Trails And Environmental Center Now Open As Park District's Largest Site Blossoms." Block Club Chicago. September 21, 2021. https://blockclubchicago.org/2021/09/21/big-marsh-parks-new-trails-and-environmental-center-now-open-as-park-districts-largest-site-expands/

21. Hunt, Nicholas. "How Mountain Biking Is Saving Small-Town, USA." *Outside*. May 15, 2017. https://www.outsideonline.com/outdoor-adventure/biking/how-mountain-biking-saving-small-town-usa/

22. Bike Cleveland, Safer Streets Campaign page. "Responses: County Executive & Council Candidate Questionnaire". Accessed July 11, 2023. https://www.bikecleveland.org/bike-cle/news/responses-county-executive-council-candidate-questionnaire/2022/04/?utm_source=rss&utm_medium=rss&utm_campaign=responses-county-executive-council-candidate-questionnaire&fbclid=IwAR37HJAWJbbz0I-fTZ6Vi1QggQHrd5E-hTSWb6CGHeH7yicLD2LxBMN-6pv9s

23. 45 Ohio Rev. Code. § 4501.01(A)(K) (2019), available at https://codes.ohio.gov/ohio-revised-code/section-4501.01

24. 45 Ohio Rev. Code. § 4511.01(A)(G) (2019), available at https://codes.ohio.gov/ohio-revised-code/section-4511.01

25. 45 Ohio Rev. Code. § 4511.07(A)(8) (2006), available at https://codes.ohio.gov/ohio-revised-code/section-4511.07

26. 45 Ohio Rev. Code. § 4511.051(A)(2) (2019), available at https://codes.ohio.gov/ohio-revised-code/section-4511.051

27. 45 Ohio Rev. Code. § 4511.01(YY) (2019), available at https://codes.ohio.gov/ohio-revised-code/section-4511.01

28. 45 Ohio Rev. Code. § 4511.711(A) (2021), available at https://codes.ohio.gov/ohio-revised-code/section-4511.711

29. "Rules of the Road for Bicyclists." City of Columbus, Ohio. Accessed April 22, 2020. https://www.columbus.gov/upload-edFiles/Columbus/Programs/Get_Active/Biking/RulesOfTh-eRoad%20(1).pdf

30. Cincinnati, Ohio, Municipal Code of Ordinances Title V-Traffic Code, Chapter 506-Operation and Right of Way, § 506-5 (1972), available at https://library.municode.com/oh/cincinnati/codes/code_of_ordinances?nodeId=TITVTR-CO_CH506OPRIWA_S506-5BIOPMI

31. "Bicycle Safety." National Highway Traffic Safety Administration (NHTSA). Accessed April 22, 2020. https://www.nhtsa.gov/sites/nhtsa.dot.gov/files/811557.pdf

32. 45 Ohio Rev. Code. § 4511.711(A) (2021), available at https://codes.ohio.gov/ohio-revised-code/section-4511.711

33. 45 Ohio Rev. Code. § 4511.441(A) (2018), available at http://codes.ohio.gov/orc/4511.441

34. Cleveland, Ohio, Municipal Code, Part Four-Traffic Code, Title IX-Pedestrians, Bicycles and Motorcycles, Chapter 473-Bicycles, Motorcycles, Mobility Devices, § 473.09(c) (2020), searchable at https://codelibrary.amlegal.com/

35. 45 Ohio Rev. Code. § 4511.07(A)(8) (2006), available at https://codes.ohio.gov/ohio-revised-code/section-4511.07

36. 45 Ohio Rev. Code. § 4511.55(B) (2019), available at https://codes.ohio.gov/ohio-revised-code/section-4511.55

37. 45 Ohio Rev. Code. § 4511.07(A)(8) (2006), available at https://codes.ohio.gov/ohio-revised-code/section-4511.07

38. 45 Ohio Rev. Code. § 4511.27(A)(1) (2018), available at https://codes.ohio.gov/ohio-revised-code/section-4511.27

39. Cleveland, Ohio, Municipal Code, Part Four-Traffic Code, Title Five-Vehicles, Chapter 431-Operation Generally, § 431.03(2)(b) (2019), searchable at https://codelibrary.amlegal.com/

40. 45 Ohio Rev. Code. § 4511.132(A)(1)(2)(3) (2018), available at https://codes.ohio.gov/ohio-revised-code/section-4511.132

41. 45 Ohio Rev. Code. § 4511.991(A)(1)(b) (2023), available at https://codes.ohio.gov/ohio-revised-code/section-4511.991

42. 45 Ohio Rev. Code. § 4511.204(A)(B)(1-13) (2023), available at https://codes.ohio.gov/ohio-revised-code/section-4511.204

43. Bishop-Henchman, Joseph. "Gasoline Taxes and User Fees Pay for Only Half of State & Local Road Spending." Tax Foundation. January 3, 2014. https://taxfoundation.org/gasoline-taxes-and-user-fees-pay-only-half-state-local-road-spending/

44. Johnson, Amanda. "Ohio lawmakers contemplate increasing gas tax to fund road repairs." *The Center Square.* February 8, 2019. https://www.thecentersquare.com/ohio/ohio-lawmakers-contemplate-increasing-gas-tax-to-fund-road-repairs/article_6305d9e6-2b02-11e9-be3f-f72a50ab46f1.html

45. Hulsey, Lynn. "Ohio's roads are rated a D. But who will pay to fix them?" *Butler County Journal-News.* February 28, 2021. https://www.journal-news.com/traffic/ohios-roads-are-rated-a-d-but-who-will-pay-to-fix-them/XSGBDHEXSZDHHP32DSQGESSW4Y/

46. "Who Pays for Roads?" Frontier Group & U.S. PIRG Education Fund, Spring 2015. https://uspirg.org/sites/pirg/files/reports/Who%20Pays%20for%20Roads%20vUS.pdf , 21.

47. Ibid., 23

48. Carlton Reid. *Roads Were Not Built for Cars,* Washington DC: 2nd edition, Island Press 2010

49. Ohio Rev. Code. § 4511.051(A)(2) (2019), available at http://codes.ohio.gov/orc/4511.051

50. 45 Ohio Rev. Code. § 4511.07(A)(8) (2006), available at https://codes.ohio.gov/ohio-revised-code/section-4511.07

51. 45 Ohio Rev. Code. § 4511.01(YY) (2023), available at https://codes.ohio.gov/ohio-revised-code/section-4511.01

52. Reid, Carlton. "Death of A 'Dinosaur:' Anti-Cycleway Campaigner John Forester Dies, Aged 90." *Forbes.* April 23, 2020. https://www.forbes.com/sites/carltonreid/2020/04/23/death-of-a-dinosaur-anti-cycleway-campaigner-john-forester-dies-aged-90/?fbclid=IwAR0EGVUs3tyvl3P30fa8c-MqL9Zq2j0EiEIXbVV2wzxb7a_WREE_Xl8-uhbc#36b42cd-51cc3

53. John Forester. *Effective Cycling,* Cambridge, MA: 7th edition, MIT Press 2012

54. 45 Ohio Rev. Code. § 4511.55(A)(C) (2019), available at https://codes.ohio.gov/ohio-revised-code/section-4511.55

55. 45 Ohio Rev. Code. § 4511.55(C) (2019), available at https://codes.ohio.gov/ohio-revised-code/section-4511.55

56. 45 Ohio Rev. Code. § 4511.52(A) (2019), available at https://codes.ohio.gov/ohio-revised-code/section-4511.52

57. 45 Ohio Rev. Code. § 4511.12(A) (2018), available at https://codes.ohio.gov/ohio-revised-code/section-4511.12

58. 45 Ohio Rev. Code. § 4511.13(C)(1)(a)(b) (2013), available at https://codes.ohio.gov/ohio-revised-code/section-4511.13

59. 45 Ohio Rev. Code. § 4511.43(A) (2018), available at https://codes.ohio.gov/ohio-revised-code/section-4511.43

60. Hilkevitch, Jon. "City says Dearborn bike signals keeping cyclists in line." *Chicago Tribune* (Chicago, Illinois), June 10, 2013. https://www.chicagotribune.com/autos/ct-xpm-2013-06-10-ct-met-getting-around-0610-20130610-story.html

61. 45 Ohio Rev. Code. § 4511.40(A)(1)(2)(3)(B) (2018), available at https://codes.ohio.gov/ohio-revised-code/section-4511.40

62. 45 Ohio Rev. Code. § 4511.39(A) (2018), available at https://codes.ohio.gov/ohio-revised-code/section-4511.39

63. 45 Ohio Rev. Code. § 4511.56(A)(1)(2)(3)(B) (2019), available at https://codes.ohio.gov/ohio-revised-code/section-4511.56

64. 45 Ohio Rev. Code. § 4511.56(A)(2)(3)(B) (2019), available at https://codes.ohio.gov/ohio-revised-code/section-4511.56

65. Bike Helmet Safety Institute, Bike Helmet Laws page. Accessed July 21, 2023. https://www.helmets.org/mandator.htm

66. Bicycle Helmet Safety Institute, Statistics page. Accessed March 17, 2019. https://helmets.org/stats.htm#effectiveness

67. U.S. Consumer Product Safety Commission. "New CDC Report Finds More Adults Are Dying from Bicycle-Related Accidents; CPSC Says it Highlights the Importance of Helmets." May 18, 2021. https://www.cpsc.gov/Newsroom/

News-Releases/2021/New-CDC-Report-Finds-More-Adults-Are-Dying-from-Bicycle-Related-Accidents-CPSC-Says-it-Highlights-the-Importance-of-Helmets

68. Delves, Joseph. "Bike helmet safety: Standards, testing and tech, plus Virginia Tech's top-rated helmets." Cyclist. June 7, 2023. https://www.cyclist.co.uk/in-depth/safest-bike-helmet

69. Mayo Foundation for Medical Education and Research (MF-MER), Post-concussion syndrome page. Accessed August 29, 2019. https://www.mayoclinic.org/diseases-conditions/post-concussion-syndrome/symptoms-causes/syc-20353352

70. Munnik, Oliver. "6 Amazing Pieces of High Visibility Cycling Gear." Bicycling. May 18, 2016. http://www.bicycling.com/bikes-gear/reviews/6-amazing-pieces-of-high-visibility-cycling-gear

71. 45 Ohio Rev. Code. § 4511.52(B)(D) (2019), available at http://codes.ohio.gov/orc/4511.52

72. 45 Ohio Rev. Code. § 4511.36(A)(2) (2018), available at https://codes.ohio.gov/ohio-revised-code/section-4511.36

73. 45 Ohio Rev. Code. § 4511.39(A) (2018), available at https://codes.ohio.gov/ohio-revised-code/section-4511.39

74. 45 Ohio Rev. Code. § 4511.36(A)(1) (2018), available at https://codes.ohio.gov/ohio-revised-code/section-4511.36

75. "Bike Boxes." National Association of Transportation Officials (NACTO). Accessed January 31, 2023. https://nacto.org/publication/urban-bikeway-design-guide/intersection-treatments/bike-boxes/

76. City of Lakewood Ohio, Biking Lakewood page. Accessed July 20, 2023. https://www.lakewoodoh.gov/bikinglakewood/

77. "Urban Bikeway Design Guide." National Association of Transportation Officials (NACTO). Accessed January 31, 2023. https://nacto.org/publication/urban-bikeway-design-guide/

78. National Association of Transportation Officials (NACTO), "Don't Give Up at the Intersection: NACTO Releases Best Practices for Next-Generation Street Intersection Design," News release, (May 20, 2019). Accessed January 31, 2023. https://nacto.org/2019/05/20/dont-give-up-at-the-intersection/?utm_source=NACTO+Newsletter&utm_campaign=a965077874-EMAIL_CAMPAIGN_2019_04_22_04_58_COPY_01&utm_medium=email&utm_term=0_8f3492144e-a965077874-1204371949&mc_cid=a965077874&mc_eid=af74595ec0

79. "Don't Give Up at the Intersection." National Association of Transportation Officials (NACTO). Accessed January 31, 2023. https://nacto.org/publication/urban-bikeway-design-guide/dont-give-up-at-the-intersection/

80. Snyder, Dave. "We Were Wrong About Sharrows." PeopleForBikes. Accessed July 20, 2023. https://www.peopleforbikes.org/news/we-were-wrong-about-sharrows?eid=126859

81. Cleveland, Ohio, Municipal Code, Part Four-Traffic Code, Title Five-Vehicles, Chapter 431-Operation Generally, § 431.08(b) (2017), searchable at https://codelibrary.amlegal.com/

82. Cleveland, Ohio, Municipal Code, Part Four-Traffic Code, Title Five-Vehicles, Chapter 451-Operation Generally, § 451.03(a)(17) (2017), searchable athttps://codelibrary.amlegal.com/

83. Cleveland, Ohio, Municipal Code Part Six-Offenses and Business Activities Code, Title l: General Offenses, Chapter

605: Disorderly Conduct and Activity, § 605.10(a)(b)(1) (2008), searchable at https://codelibrary.amlegal.com/

84. Haidet, Ryan. "Dog attacks and postal workers: Cleveland ranks No. 4 nationwide according to USPS data." Updated June 2, 2023. https://www.wkyc.com/article/news/local/cleveland/united-states-postal-service-mail-carriers-mail-men-dog- attacks/95-b8e4ba3f-0226-4175-ba18-0a969ad-3c6c2

85. 9 Ohio Rev. Code. § 955.261(A)(2)(3), available at: https://codes.ohio.gov/ohio-revised-code/section-955.261

86. U.S. Department of Homeland Security. Stop the Bleed page. Accessed July 24, 2023. https://www.dhs.gov/publication/stop-bleed-tourniquet

87. Hurford, Molly. "How To Draft While Cycling for More Efficient Riding." Bicycling. November 22, 2021. https://www.bicycling.com/skills-tips/a38238367/how-to-draft-while-cycling/

88. Cleveland Metroparks, Home page. Accessed July 24, 2023. https://www.clevelandmetroparks.com/

89. Bialick, Aaron. "Wiggle Riders to Show Folly of Stop Sign Law By Complying With It." Streetsblog SF, July 27, 2015. https://sf.streetsblog.org/2015/07/27/wiggle-riders-to-show-folly-of-stop-sign-law-by-complying-with-it/

90. 45 Ohio Rev. Code. § 4511.31(B)(1)(2)(3) (2018), available at http://codes.ohio.gov/orc/4511.31

91. 45 Ohio Rev. Code. § 4511.27(A)(1) (2018), available at https://codes.ohio.gov/ohio-revised-code/section-4511.27

92. 45 Ohio Rev. Code. § 4511.28(A)(2) (2018), available at https://codes.ohio.gov/ohio-revised-code/section-4511.28

93. Schmitt, Angie. "Arkansas Passes the 'Idaho Stop,' Allowing Cyclists to Treat Red Lights Like Stop Signs." Streetsblog USA, April 3, 2019. https://usa.streetsblog.org/2019/04/03/the-idaho-stop-is-finally-starting-to-happen/

94. Schmitt, Angie. "Oregon Legislature Passes 'Idaho Stop' Bill." Streetsblog USA, June 27, 2019. https://usa.streetsblog.org/2019/06/27/idaho-stop-passes-in-oregon

95. Bicycle Retailer, Industry News page. "Washington state will be latest to enact Safety Stop Law." September 30, 2020. https://www.bicycleretailer.com/industry-news/2020/09/30/washington-state-latest-pass-safety-stop-law#.YFdrPC1h2fS

96. Bicycle Retailer, Industry News page. "Oklahoma passes Idaho Stop law, joining growing list of states." May 11, 2021. https://www.bicycleretailer.com/industry-news/2021/05/11/oklahoma-passes-idaho-stop-law

97. Bicycle Retailer, Industry News page. "Utah, North Dakota latest to adopt safety stop law for cyclists." March 30, 2021. https://www.bicycleretailer.com/industry-news/2021/03/21/utah-latest-adopt-safety-stop-law-cyclists#.Ygqy0d_MKM8

98. Sanchez, Jared. "Bicycle Safety Stop Bill Passes Senate." California Bicycle Coalition (CalBike). August 31, 2021. https://www.calbike.org/bicycle-safety-stop-bill-passes-senate/

99. Greenfield, John. "Illinois lawmakers killed an 'Idaho stop' bill this week, but one could pass in the future." Streetsblog Chicago. February 17, 2022. https://chi.streetsblog.org/2022/02/17/illinois-lawmakers-killed-an-idaho-stop-bill-this-week-but-one-could-pass-in-the-future/

100. "Every Life Counts: Improving the Safety of Our Nation's Roadways." National Transportation Board (NTSB). Accessed August 24, 2023. https://www.ntsb.gov/news/speeches/JHomendy/Documents/homendy-20190409.pdf

101. "Ohio Distracted Driving Task Force Report FINAL," Govdelivery. Accessed August 24, 2023. https://content. govdelivery.com/attachments/OHOOD/2019/04/24/file_attachments/1198896/Ohio%20Distracted%20Driving%20 Task%20Force%20Report%20FINAL.pdf

102. Ohio State Highway Patrol, Distracted Driving Dashboard page. Accessed August 2, 2023. https://statepatrol.ohio.gov/ dashboards-statistics/ostats-dashboards/distracted-driving-dashboard

103. Leicht, Angelica. "Texting And Driving Statistics 2023." Forbes ADVISOR. Updated January 3, 2023. https://www. forbes.com/advisor/car-insurance/texting-driving-statistics/#:~:text=When%20you%20send%20or%20read%20 a%20text%2C%20you,of%20a%20football%20field%20 with%20your%20eyes%20shut

104. 45 Ohio Rev. Code. § 4511.991(A)(1)(b) (2023), available at https://codes.ohio.gov/ohio-revised-code/section-4511.991

105. 45 Ohio Rev. Code. § 4511.204(A)(B)(1-13) (2023), available at https://codes.ohio.gov/ohio-revised-code/section-4511.204

106. 45 Ohio Rev. Code § 4511.70(C) (2004), available at http:// codes.ohio.gov/orc/4511.70

107. Governors Highway Safety Association, "New Projection: U.S. Pedestrian Deaths Jumped in First Half of 2021." News release, (April 7, 2022). Accessed August 3, 2023. https:// www.ghsa.org/resources/news-releases/GHSA/Ped-Spotlight22

108. Ohio State Highway Patrol, Traffic Safety Bulletin page. Accessed August 3, 2023. https://statepatrol.ohio.gov/static/ links/Pedestrian_Bulletin_2022.pdf

109. Vision Zero Cleveland, Crash Maps & Data page. Accessed August 3, 2023. https://www.visionzerocle.org/pages/data

110. Bailey v. Vaughn, 8th Dist. Cuyahoga No. 105412, 2017-Ohio-7725

111. GoPro, Inc., Cameras page. Accessed August 3, 2023. https://shop.gopro.com/cameras

112. Knabe Law Firm Co. L.P.A., Home page. Accessed August 3, 2023. http://klfohio.com/

113. Brouhard, Rod. "An Overview of Traumatic Brain Injury." VeryWellHealth, updated April 22, 2022. https://www.verywellhealth.com/difference-between-concussions-and-traumatic-brain-injuries-4126107

114. Rosenthal, Michele. "The Science Behind PTSD Symptoms: How Trauma Changes The Brain." *PsychCentral,* updated July 2, 2021. https://psychcentral.com/blog/the-science-behind-ptsd-symptoms-how-trauma-changes-the-brain/

115. Ohio City Incorporated, Home page. Accessed August 3, 2023. https://www.ohiocity.org/ohiocityincorporated

116. MidTown Cleveland, Staff page. Accessed August 3, 2023. https://midtowncleveland.org/staff/

117. With permission of Ashley Shaw.

118. Velosurance, Free Instant Quote page. Accessed August 3, 2023. https://velosurance.com

119. State v. Patrick, 153 Ohio Misc. 2d 20, 2008-Ohio-7142, 914 N.E.2d 1121, 2008 Ohio Misc. LEXIS 311

120. State v. Gatto, 2007-Ohio-4609, 2007 Ohio App. LEXIS 4154

121. State v. Tudor, 2019-Ohio-24, 118 N.E.3d 297, 2019 Ohio App. LEXIS 25, 2019 WL 117947

122. State v. Copley, 2010-Ohio-2340, 2010 Ohio App. LEXIS 1932, 2010 WL 2106015

123. Cummings v. Lyles, 2015-Ohio-316, 27 N.E.3d 985, 2015 Ohio App. LEXIS 275

124. Passwaters v. Knaur, 2006-Ohio-1518, 2006 Ohio App. LEXIS 1419

125. Deutsch v. Birk, 189 Ohio App. 3d 129, 2010-Ohio-3564, 937 N.E.2d 638, 2010 Ohio App. LEXIS 3024

126. Crabtree v. Cook, 196 Ohio App. 3d 546, 2011-Ohio-5612, 964 N.E.2d 473, 2011 Ohio App. LEXIS 4604, 2011 WL 5184196

127. 15 Ohio Rev. Code. § 1533.18 (2007), available at https://codes.ohio.gov/ohio-revised-code/section-1533.18

128. 15 Ohio Rev. Code. § 1533.181 (1995), available at https://codes.ohio.gov/ohio-revised-code/section-1533.181

129. Storc v. Day Drive Assocs. Ltd., 2006-Ohio-561, 2006 Ohio App. LEXIS 495

130. Kane v. City of Dayton, Montgomery Cty. C.P. Ct. No. 2017-CV-04722 (2018)

131. Bailey v. Vaughn, 2017-Ohio-7725, 2017 Ohio App. LEXIS 4121, 2017 WL 4176996

132. "USDOT Releases New Data Showing That Road Fatalities Spiked in First Half of 2021." National Highway Traffic Safety Administration (NHTSA). October 28, 2021. https://www.nhtsa.gov/press-releases/usdot-releases-new-data-showing-road-fatalities-spiked-first-half-2021

133. "U.S. Transportation Secretary Pete Buttigieg Announces Comprehensive National Roadway Safety Strategy." U.S.

Department of Transportation (USDOT). January 27, 2022. https://www.transportation.gov/briefing-room/us-trans-portation-secretary-pete-buttigieg-announces-comprehen-sive-national-roadway

134. Pagonakis, Joe. "In-Depth: Bicycle crashes, deaths climbing across Ohio." News 5 Cleveland. Updated May 20, 2021. https://www.news5cleveland.com/news/local-news/in-depth/in-depth-bicycle-crashes-deaths-climbing-across-ohio

135. Vision Zero Cleveland, Data Insights page. Accessed August 4, 2023. https://www.visionzerocle.org/pages/data

136. Advocates for Highway and Auto Safety, 2022 Roadmap of State Highway Safety Laws page. Accessed August 4, 2023. https://saferoads.org/wp-content/uploads/2022/01/FINAL-2022-Roadmap-of-State-Highway-Safety-Laws.pdf

137. 45 Ohio Rev. Code. § 4511.204(A)(B)(1-13) (2023), available at https://codes.ohio.gov/ohio-revised-code/sec-tion-4511.204

138. 45 Ohio Rev. Code. § 4511.991(A)(1)(b) (2023), available at https://codes.ohio.gov/ohio-revised-code/section-4511.991

139. The League of American Bicyclists, Report Cards page. Accessed August 4, 2023. https://bikeleague.org/bfa/states/state-report-cards/

140. Spin Bike Shop, Home page. Accessed August 8, 2023. https://www.spinbikeshop.com/

141. Gear Up Velo, Home page. Accessed August 8, 2023. https://www.gearupvelo.com/

142. Electric Pete's E-bikes, Home page. Accessed August 8, 2023. https://electricpete.com/

143. "100 Bird e-bikes arriving in Cleveland, joining existing fleet of e-scooters." News 5 Cleveland. Updated March 21, 2022. https://www.news5cleveland.com/news/local-news/cleveland-metro/100-bird-e-bikes-arriving-in-cleveland-joining-existing-fleet-of-e-scooters

144. Allard, Sam. "Bird adds 100 e-bikes to Cleveland Scooter Fleet." March 23, 2022. https://www.clevescene.com/news/bird-adds-100-e-bikes-to-cleveland-scooter-fleet-38596894

145. "E-Bike Laws in the USA by State: Overview of Electric Bike Regulations." eBike Generation. Accessed August 9, 2023. https://ebikegeneration.com/pages/e-bike-laws-in-the-usa-by-state

146. Richtel, Matt. "'A Dangerous Combination': Teenagers' Accidents Expose E-Bike Risks." Updated July 30, 2023. https://www.nytimes.com/2023/07/29/health/ebikes-safety-teens.html?smid=nytcore-ios-share&referringSource=articleShare

147. PeopleForBikes and the League of American Bicyclists. "E-Bike Smart: Your Guide to Safe Riding." Accessed September 12, 2023. https://www.ebikesmart.org/

148. E-bike battery recycling, Hungry for Trash E-Bike Batteries page. Accessed September 12, 2023. https://www.hungryfor-batteries.org/?eid=130255

149. The Ohio Legislature. House Bill 250 Summary page. Accessed August 10, 2023. https://www.legislature.ohio.gov/legislation/132/hb250

150. "State Electric Bicycle Laws | A Legislative Primer." National Conference of State Legislatures. Updated February 24, 2021. https://www.ncsl.org/research/transportation/state-electric-bicycle-laws-a-legislative-primer.aspx

151. 45 Ohio Rev. Code § 4511.01(TTT) (2019), available at
https://codes.ohio.gov/ohio-revised-code/section-4511.01

152. 45 Ohio Rev. Code § 4511.01(UUU) (2019), available at
https://codes.ohio.gov/ohio-revised-code/section-4511.01

153. 45 Ohio Rev. Code § 4511.01(VVV) (2019), available at
https://codes.ohio.gov/ohio-revised-code/section-4511.01

154. 45 Ohio Rev. Code § 4511.522 (D)(2)(2019), available at
https://codes.ohio.gov/ohio-revised-code/section-4511.522

155. 45 Ohio Rev. Code § 4511.522 (D)(1)(2019), available at
https://codes.ohio.gov/ohio-revised-code/section-4511.522

156. "Can I Ride My E-Bike There?" Bike Cleveland. Accessed
September 13, 2023. https://www.bikecleveland.org/bike-cle/
news/e-bike/2018/12/?fbclid=IwAR0D_GV[D3l7RKXQa-
SQ1nxyadJjlKXiwT96vGqN_f8JvTIUyM18lzyQrkHLg

157. 45 Ohio Rev. Code § 4511.522(C)(1) (2019), available at
https://codes.ohio.gov/ohio-revised-code/section-4511.522

158. 45 Ohio Rev. Code § 4511.522(C)(2) (2019), available at
https://codes.ohio.gov/ohio-revised-code/section-4511.522

159. 45 Ohio Rev. Code § 4511.522(C)(3) (2019), available at
http://codes.ohio.gov/orc/4511.522

160. "Bicycle Safety." National Highway Traffic Safety Administration (NHTSA). Accessed August 8, 2023. https://www.nhtsa.
gov/sites/nhtsa.dot.gov/files/811557.pdf

161. The League of American Bicyclists, Products page. Accessed
August 11, 2023. https://shop.bikeleague.org/products/
youth-skills-instructors-manual

162. "AASHTO Guide for the Planning, Design, and Operation of
Bicycle Facilities." American Association of State Highway

and Transportation Officials. Accessed September 5, 2023. https://www.albany.edu/ihi/files/DraftBikeGuideFeb2010.pdf

163. Wander, Mitch. "Parallel stormwater grates can endanger cyclists. If you see one, say something." Greater Greater Washington (GGWash). April 20, 2018. https://ggwash.org/view/67323/see-some-stormwater-grates-that-could-endanger-cyclists-let-dc-water-know

164. Ohio Department of Transportation (ODOT), On-Road Bicycle Facilities page. July 21, 2023. https://www.transportation.ohio.gov/working/engineering/roadway/manuals-standards/multimodal/06/06#62BicycleRoutes

165. Knabe Law Firm, Julie Notice page. Accessed August 11, 2023. https://klfohio.com/letter/

166. Bike Cleveland, Home page. Accessed August 12, 2023. https://www.bikecleveland.org/

167. Bike Cleveland, Resources page. Accessed August 12, 2023. https://www.bikecleveland.org/resources/getting-around-bike

168. Greater Cleveland Regional Transit Authority, Rack-N-Roll with GCRTA page. Accessed August 12, 2023. https://www.riderta.com/racknroll

169. Ohio City Bicycle Co-op, Home page. Accessed August 12, 2023. https://ohiocitycycles.org

170. Ohio Bicycle Federation, Home page. Accessed August 12, 2023. https://www.ohiobike.org/

171. Ohio to Erie Trail, Home page. Accessed August 14, 2023. https://www.ohiotoerietrail.org/content.aspx?page_id=0&club_id=146576

172. Ohio to Erie Trail, Board of Directors page. Accessed August 14, 2023. https://www.ohiotoerietrail.org/content.aspx?page_id=22&club_id=146576&module_id=542121

173. Ohio to Erie Trail, Trail Shop page. Accessed August 14, 2023. https://ohiotoerietrail.org/shop

174. Ohio & Erie Canal Towpath Trail/Ohio To Erie Trail Enthusiasts Group. Facebook. Accessed August 14, 2023. https://www.facebook.com/groups/365793010917596

175. Ohio to Erie Trail, Plan Your Trip page. Accessed August 14, 2023. https://ohiotoerietrail.org/content.aspx?page_id=22&club_id=146576&module_id=533398

176. Ohio to Erie Trail, Interactive Map and Resources page. Accessed August 14, 2023. https://ohiotoerietrail.org/content.aspx?page_id=22&club_id=146576&module_id=505037

177. Ohio to Erie Trail, GPS Navigation Links page. Accessed August 14, 2023. https://ohiotoerietrail.org/OTET_RWGPS

178. Daris, Lisa. "Mike Groeber, our master adjuster." Ohio to Erie Trail. December 17, 2022. https://www.ohiotoerietrail.org/content.aspx?page_id=5&club_id=146576&item_id=82694

179. Ohio to Erie Trail, Board of Directors page. Accessed August 14, 2023. https://www.ohiotoerietrail.org/content.aspx?page_id=22&club_id=146576&module_id=542121

180. Akron Bicycling Club, Home page. Accessed August 15, 2023. https://akronbike.org/content.aspx?page_id=0&club_id=133645

181. Cleveland Touring Club, Home page. Accessed August 15, 2023. https://www.clevelandtouringclub.org/

182. Hudson Velo, Home page. Accessed August 15, 2023. https://hudsonvelo.clubexpress.com/content.aspx?page_id=4&club_id=700705

183. Lake Erie Wheelers, Home page. Accessed August 15, 2023. https://www.lakeeriewheelers.org/

184. Lorain County Bicycle Club, Home page. Accessed August 15, 2023. https://loraincountybicycleclub.org/

185. Silver Wheels Cycling Club, Home page. Accessed August 16, 2023. https://silverwheelscyclingclub.wildapricot.org/

186. Slow Roll Cleveland, Home page. Accessed August 16, 2023. https://www.slowrollcleveland.org/

187. Stark County Bicycle Club, Home page. Accessed August 16, 2023. http://bikescbc.com/index.shtml

188. Congressman Jimmy Panetta. "REPS. PANETTA, BLUMENAUER, THOMPSON, AND SCHIFF REINTRODUCE E-BIKE ACT." Press release, (March 21, 2023). Accessed August 16, 2023. https://panetta.house.gov/media/press-releases/reps-panetta-blumenauer-thompson-and-schiff-reintroduce-e-bike-act

189. Senate Committee on Energy & Natural Resources. "Manchin, Barrasso Introduce Bipartisan America's Outdoor Recreation Act." News release, (March 16, 2023). Accessed August 17, 2023. https://www.energy.senate.gov/2023/3/manchin-barrasso-introduce-bipartisan-america-s-outdoor-recreation-act

190. "Governor DeWine Signs Bill that Strengthens Distracted Driving Laws in Ohio." News release, (January 03, 2023). Accessed August 17, 2023. https://governor.ohio.gov/media/news-and-media/governor-dewine-signs-bill-that-strengthens-distracted-driving-laws-in-ohio-01032023

191. Cleveland Metropolitan School District, Wellness/Safe Routes to School page. Accessed August 17, 2023. https://www.clevelandmetroschools.org/saferoutes

192. Cleveland City Council. "Cleveland City Council Final Meeting Highlights (6/6/22)." June 6, 2022. https://www.clevelandcitycouncil.org/resources/news-media/cleveland-city-council-final-meeting-highlights-6622

193. "Cleveland streets to include more multi-modal, environmentally-friendly designs under strengthened Complete and Green Streets policy." Cleveland.com. Updated June 6, 2022. https://www.cleveland.com/news/2022/06/cleveland-streets-to-include-more-multi-modal-environmentally-friendly-designs-under-strengthened-complete-and-green-streets-policy.html

194. Litt, Steven. "NOACA announces $44.8M in grants, including a big boost for Cleveland's Midway and Lorain Avenue cycle track." Cleveland.com. Updated January 21, 2022. https://www.cleveland.com/news/2022/01/noaca-announces-448m-in-grants-including-a-big-boost-for-clevelands-midway-and-lorain-avenue-cycle-track.html

195. Astolfi, Courtney. "Cleveland advances plan to add 4-plus miles of protected bikes lanes on Superior, Lorain avenues." Cleveland.com. Updated: January 12, 2023. https://www.cleveland.com/news/2023/01/cleveland-advances-plan-to-add-4-plus-miles-of-protected-bikes-lanes-on-superior-lorain-avenues.html

196. Cleveland City Council. "Council's Development, Planning and Sustainability Committee Approves Superior and Lorain Midway Ordinances at January 17 Committee Meeting." January 17, 2023. https://www.clevelandcitycouncil.org/councils-development-planning-and-sustainability-committee-approves-superior-and-lorain-midway

197. Eaton, Sabrina. "Massive year-end spending bill includes new Great Lakes Authority and other Ohio priorities." Cleveland.com. Updated March 7, 2023. https://www.cleveland.com/news/2022/12/massive-year-end-spending-bill-includes-new-great-lakes-authority-and-other-ohio-priorities.html

198. Trau, Morgan. "Cleveland's Superior Midway bike project saved after backlash." News5 Cleveland. Updated February 22, 2023. https://www.news5cleveland.com/news/politics/ohio-politics/clevelands-superior-midway-bike-project-saved-after-backlash

199. Litt, Steven. "NOACA announces $44.8M in grants, including a big boost for Cleveland's Midway and Lorain Avenue cycle track." Cleveland.com. Updated January 21, 2022. https://www.cleveland.com/news/2022/01/noaca-announces-448m-in-grants-including-a-big-boost-for-clevelands-midway-and-lorain-avenue-cycle-track.html

200. Bike Cleveland, Data Insights page. Accessed August 18, 2023. https://www.visionzerocle.org/pages/data

201. The Law Firm for Truck Safety LLP, Home page. Accessed August 18, 2023. https://truckaccidents.com/

202. Vision Zero Cleveland, Home page. Accessed September 21, 2023. https://www.visionzerocle.org/

203. 45 Ohio Rev. Code § 4511.01(A)(G) (2019), available at https://codes.ohio.gov/ohio-revised-code/section-4511.01

KNABE LAW FIRM L.P.A.

14222 MADISON AVENUE
LAKEWOOD, OH 44107

216-228-7200

WWW.KLFOHIO.COM

WA